SUMMARY

Since the end of the Cold War, the United States has intervened in the affairs of sovereign states on several occasions by using military force. A combination of humanitarian sentiments and practical policy considerations motivated both Democratic and Republican presidents to become involved in civil wars and humanitarian crises. These interventions met with mixed results, and even the most successful missions encountered serious problems. Improving the conduct of such interventions requires understanding these past operations as well as considering conflicts in which the United States chose not to intervene.

This Letort Paper covers U.S. military interventions in civil conflicts since the end of the Cold War. It defines intervention as the use of military force to achieve a specific objective (i.e., deliver humanitarian aid, support revolutionaries or insurgents, protect a threatened population, etc.) and focuses on the phase of the intervention in which kinetic operations occurred. The Paper considers five conflicts in which the United States intervened: Somalia (1992-93), Haiti (1994), Bosnia (1995), Kosovo (1999), and Libya (2011). It also reviews two crises in which Washington might have intervened but chose not to: Rwanda (1994) and Syria (2011-12). The author examines each case using five broad analytical questions: 1. Could the intervention have achieved its objective at an acceptable cost in blood and treasure? 2. What policy considerations prompted the intervention? 3. How did the United States intervene? 4. Was the intervention followed by a Phase 4 stability operation? and 5. Did Washington have a viable exit strategy?

i

Answering these questions reveals distinct patterns in U.S. interventions. Despite their frequent reference to American values, Presidents have rarely intervened on purely humanitarian grounds. Some strategic interest usually underlay even the most seemingly altruistic missions. Although they had the means to intervene unilaterally, every administration sought international approval for intervention and usually entered a threatened state as part of a coalition, often one made up of North Atlantic Treaty Organization allies. Whenever possible, the United States sought to intervene with airpower alone. It avoided deploying ground troops, and when it did so, made sure that those forces operated under robust rules of engagement with rigorous force protection pursuing limited objectives unlikely to cause casualties. A United Nations Peacekeeping Mission usually followed American interventions, and the Pentagon always insisted that developing a viable exit strategy be part of the planning process for each mission, although this requirement was not always met.

From the patterns evident in past campaigns lessons to inform the conduct of future missions can be derived. The United States should only intervene when doing so has a reasonable chance of success. When intervention becomes necessary, the White House should seek international approval and operate as part of a coalition or alliance with airpower being its primary contribution. If it must deploy ground troops, it should keep the American footprint small and withdraw forces as soon as possible.

AVOIDING THE SLIPPERY SLOPE: CONDUCTING EFFECTIVE INTERVENTIONS

INTRODUCTION

Operation ODYSSEY DAWN was but the latest in a series of problematic humanitarian interventions in which American forces have participated over the past 20 years. Since the end of the Cold War, the United States has intervened in Somalia (1992-93), Haiti (1994-95), Bosnia (1995-2004), Kosovo (1999-present), and Libya (2011). In each case, the White House waited until a crisis was well advanced, assembled or joined a coalition of the (often reluctantly) willing, and employed force in a tentative, circumscribed manner. Such an approach rarely produced decisive results in a timely fashion. Failure to clearly define mission goals along with consistently underestimating the difficulty of the task has often led to waste and mission creep.

Even the most recent, successful intervention in Libya was fraught with difficulties. The North Atlantic Treaty Organization (NATO) air campaign in support of rebel ground forces succeeded in ending Muammar Qaddafi's reign of terror, but it took far longer than anticipated and faced mounting opposition in the United States and abroad. The nature and stability of the new regime over the long run will shape conclusions about the success or failure of the mission. The operation also raised disturbing political and moral questions. Why, critics asked, intervene to protect innocent civilians in Libya while ignoring their plight in Bahrain, Yemen, and especially Syria? As the death toll in Syria rises, cries for intervention mount matched by adamant refusals by both China and Russia to sanction what they see as meddling in the internal affairs of a sovereign state. Since Libya

1

has oil while Syria does not, cynics have claimed that economic self-interest rather than humanitarian sentiment determines when and where the United States will act.

This mixed record of U.S.-led interventions, coupled with their unpopularity at home, suggests two options for the future: cease humanitarian intervention altogether or learn to intervene more effectively. Given that humanitarian missions are wars of choice fought for allegedly altruistic reasons, as opposed to wars of necessity waged in response to a direct threat, future administrations could refuse to get involved in the affairs of other states, no matter how badly governments treat their own people. American history and values, however, suggest that complete aloofness in the face of suffering will never be established policy. We cannot intervene always and everywhere, but we will certainly intervene at certain times and places. Deciding where, when, and how to intervene is the challenge all Presidents face. Such decisions may be guided by analysis of interventions during the past 2 decades within the context of broader U.S. military history and in light of previous studies on the subject of military intervention.

MILITARY INTERVENTION IN U.S. HISTORY

The United States has a long history of foreign military intervention. No sooner had the country emerged as a player on the stage of world affairs following the Spanish American War than it began to project power abroad. It has continued to intervene in the affairs of foreign states ever since. The nature of that intervention has, however, changed over the past century. Leaving aside major conventional wars, the history of foreign military involvement falls roughly into three periods: the era of gunboat diplomacy from 1900 to 1945; the era of the Cold War, 1945-89; and the post-Cold War world, 1989 to the present. Domestic conditions and international circumstances in each era determined when, where, and how the United States conducted interventions.

Era of Gunboat Diplomacy.

During the era of gunboat diplomacy, the United States generally confined its foreign military involvement to the small, unofficial empire it had acquired during the Spanish American War and to a self-proclaimed sphere of influence in the Caribbean and Central America. It did, however, contribute approximately 3,500 Soldiers and Marines to a coalition suppressing the Boxer Rebellion in China in 1900. The U.S. military's first experience with modern counterinsurgency came in the Philippines. From 1899 to 1902, American forces suppressed an insurgency through a combination of small-unit counterguerrilla operations and economic and political initiatives that would later be called "winning hearts and minds."[1]

While suppressing the Philippine insurrection represented consolidating control of an American protectorate, operations in the Caribbean and Central America involved intervening in the affairs of sovereign states, sometimes with, sometimes without the consent of their governments. In 1914, U.S. Marines captured and held the Mexican city of Veracruz in response to the arrest of American Sailors by the city's police. Following a raid against Columbus, New Mexico, on March 9, 1916, by Mexican bandit/revolutionary Francisco "Poncho" Villa, President Woodrow

Wilson sent a U.S. Army expedition across the border to pursue him. The operation continued until February 1915, inflicting casualties on Villa's paramilitary organization without capturing its leader.

During the interwar period, U.S. forces also intervened in the Caribbean and Latin America. For about a year beginning in February 1929, Marine Captain Merritt "Red Mike" Edson conducted counterinsurgency operations against Nicaraguan revolutionary Augusto Sandino in support of the American-backed government in Managua. Though they failed to capture Sandino, Edson's operations along the Rio Coco became the stuff of Marine Corps legend, and his writings contributed to the Corps' *Small Wars Manual*.[2] Desire to assure payment of debts to American investors led to military occupation of the Dominican Republic from 1916 to 1924.[3] A combination of economic interests and desire to reduce French and German involvement in the country motivated President Woodrow Wilson to begin an occupation of Haiti that lasted from 1915 to 1934.[4]

Intervention during the era of gunboat diplomacy generally followed a distinct pattern. All interventions, with the exception of the Boxer Rebellion, were unilateral. With the exception of the Philippine operation conducted to secure a de facto colony acquired after the Spanish American War and the brief mission to China during the Boxer Rebellion, interventions occurred within the American sphere of influence in the Caribbean and Latin America. As the terms "gunboat diplomacy" and "dollar diplomacy" (used almost interchangeably during this era) suggest, the U.S. intervened to protect American economic interests and to prevent European powers increasing their influence in the region. The building of the Panama

Canal increased the strategic importance of the Caribbean, whose islands the United States viewed as an
outer defense perimeter for the vital waterway. All of
these interventions, with the exception of the Philippines, involved a small number of U.S. troops from
an all-volunteer force. While policy debates occurred
around some of the interventions, none of them
became a serious public relations problem for any
administration in Washington.

The Cold War.

From 1941 to 1945, the United States was, of
course, preoccupied with World War II. The emerging
ideological struggle with the Soviet Union and later
China prevented a return to the Western Hemisphere
isolationism of the prewar period. The advent of the
Cold War began a new period of interventionism.
From 1946 to 1949, U.S. forces helped the Greek government defeat a communist insurgency using largely
conventional means.[5] During the same period, American advisors aided the government of the Philippines
in suppressing the Communist Hukbalahap Revolt
(1946-54), which, like the conflict in Greece, was won
through use of superior military force.[6] American
forces leading a United Nations (UN) enforcement
mission repelled a communist invasion of South
Korea in 1950 and then engaged China in a desultory
3-year war that resulted in a return to the *status quo
ante*. From July to October 1958, U.S. forces supported
the government of Lebanon against rebels as part of
the "Eisenhower Doctrine," a policy of preventing
Soviet infiltration into the Middle East.[7] In 1965, the
administration of Lyndon Johnson sent troops into the
Dominican Republic to help defeat an insurgency that
threatened to make the island another Cuba.[8]

5

Vietnam represented the largest intervention of the Cold War. Beginning as an advisory mission in 1956, the conflict escalated to a major war, drawing in 543,000 U.S. troops, only 80,000 of whom were combat Soldiers, and eventually costing billions of dollars and the lives of 58,000 Americans.[9] Unlike any previous intervention, Vietnam was a hybrid war involving a conventional conflict across the demilitarized zone between North and South Vietnam and insurgency waged in the Vietnamese countryside.[10] Despite some notable success with Combined Action Platoons to protect local communities, Civil Operations and Rural Development Support to win hearts and minds, and the Phoenix program aimed at destroying the Viet Cong leadership, the United States never mounted an effective counterinsurgency campaign. Rising costs and growing opposition to the war among the American public led to withdrawal in 1973, followed by the collapse of the South Vietnamese government in 1975.

The Vietnam War did not end American interventionism during the Cold War, but it profoundly affected how intervention took place. Even before the conflict in Southeast Asia had ended, President Richard Nixon defined a new approach to aiding threatened governments. "We shall furnish military and economic assistance to our allies in accordance with our treaty commitments," the President declared in a November 3, 1969, speech on the island of Guam. "But we shall look to the nation directly threatened to assume the primary responsibility of providing the manpower for its defense."[11] The Nixon doctrine developed into what came to be called assistance for "foreign internal defense."[12]

Assistance for foreign internal defense provided the model for a major intervention during the 1980s.

Small teams of advisors from the Special Forces supported the government of El Salvador in its decade-long struggle against the Farabundo Marti National Liberation Front (FMLN), a Marxist insurgent group. At the same time, the United States covertly supported Contra insurgents against the Sandinista government of Nicaragua. The Sandinistas fell from power, and the Salvadoran Civil War was brought to an end through a strategy of co-option. With American support, the Salvadoran government prevented the insurgents from seizing power, but it had to accede to some of their demands and bring them into the legitimate political process.[13]

Some larger operations still occurred during this period. In 1983, President Ronald Reagan sent Marines to Lebanon for what proved to be a disastrous, short-lived mission. He invaded Grenada that same year to prevent the spread of Cuban influence in the Caribbean, and in 1986 authorized the bombing of Libya in retaliation for terrorist attacks in Europe. In 1989, President George H. W. Bush invaded Panama to remove the dictator Manuel Noriega. Most of these missions, however, involved use of conventional forces in a short, sharp, decisive operation. When the Marine contingent in Beirut suffered a devastating terrorist attack, the President withdrew them almost at once.

Cold War interventions differed markedly from those during the era of gunboat diplomacy in one striking respect: ideology surpassed economics as the major reason for intervention. American Presidents cast virtually all interventions as anti-communist crusades. They even justified interventions in the Caribbean and Latin America, Washington's historic sphere of influence, on altruistic grounds. "One compelling aspect of U.S. foreign policy during the cold war," Michael Butler concluded, "was the propensity of policy makers to seek harmony between the pursuit of security objectives and a stated American belief in enduring values of peace and justice."[14] This altruistic approach led to an increasing desire to clothe unilateralism in the guise of a multilateral approach. Korea was a UN-sanctioned mission, and the Southeast Asian Treaty Organization supported the Vietnam War. Even the intervention in the Dominican Republic enjoyed nominal support from the Organization of American States (OAS). Concerns over unilateralism and legitimacy may in turn have been influenced by the greater public scrutiny of events made possible by the advent of television.

Despite these changes, interventions during the Cold War exhibited some consistency with those mounted during the era of gunboat diplomacy. The United States still showed a marked preference to send advisors rather than combat troops. The interventions in Greece, the Philippines, El Salvador, and Nicaragua were conducted with small military assistance groups or covert operatives. Even the Vietnam War began with the U.S. military in an advisory role. In those cases in which the United States sent in larger contingents, the White House withdrew them as quickly as possible. Korea (defense against a conventional invasion) and Vietnam (a hybrid war) were the exceptions, not the rule.

The Post-Cold War Era.

The opening of the Berlin Wall in 1989 and the collapse of the Soviet Union 2 years later profoundly changed the international security environment in ways that are still playing out. The end of the Cold War reduced the likelihood of a nuclear holocaust but increased exponentially the risk of small wars and insurgencies around the globe. The vacuum created by the withdrawal of Soviet power from Eastern Europe, Asia, and Africa, followed by a concomitant reduction of the U.S. presence in those areas, contributed to local and regional instability.

The increase in civil conflicts and the thaw in U.S.-Russian relations created numerous opportunities for intervention while changing the circumstances in which interventions might occur. The end of the Cold War deadlock in the Security Council meant that the UN could approve more peace operations and that the United States would be able to participate in them. This increased ability to sanction missions created a strong impression that without UN approval, intervention lacked legitimacy. As a result, the United States would seek UN approval, even when it intervened in its historic sphere of influence.

Both the United States and the UN asserted their new role in international affairs. Success in the brief, decisive Gulf War (1991) emboldened the United States to become involved in missions it might not otherwise have undertaken. For its part, the UN saw an opportunity to extend peacekeeping into the realm of civil conflict. UN Secretary-General Boutros Boutros-Ghali's *Agenda for Peace* declared that the era of absolute national sovereignty had ended and made a powerful case for humanitarian intervention.[15] This statement would provide the ideological and legal justification for the large missions of the 1990s.

The end of the Cold War also removed a major ideological justification for intervention. Opposing the spread of communism would no longer serve as a pretext for action or a legitimate foreign policy objective. At the same time, protecting human rights and preventing human catastrophes became valid reasons for intervening in the affairs of a sovereign state. Naked self-interest remained a strong motivator for action abroad, but it had to be clothed in the guise of altruism. Coupled with a communications revolution that created the Internet and mobile phones, this humanitarian imperative created a new challenge for Washington. Moved by heart-rending images of suffering on television, the public might call for humanitarian intervention. Seeing images of American casualties, that same public might quickly demand withdrawal of U.S. forces.

The United States thus faced a more complex security environment with many more opportunities to intervene. At the same time, American Presidents had to deal with a more informed public, which could constrain its ability to act. These conditions have persisted to the present and will remain for the foreseeable future. Deciding when, where, and how to intervene effectively will remain as a major challenge facing successive administrations. Such determination may be facilitated by careful analysis of the interventions that have occurred during the post-Cold War era, which differs significantly from previous eras.

The Literature of Intervention.

Intervention during the post-Cold War era has been the subject of considerable study. A spate of works cover the big UN missions of the 1990s. Most of these focus on specific conflicts, but a few broad analytical works deserve mention. Paul Diehl's *International Peacekeeping* and William Durch's *The Evolution of UN Peacekeeping* provide broad analytical studies with analysis of comparative cases, as does Thomas Mockaitis' *Peace Operations and Intra-state Conflict*.[16]

A few studies have examined the generic challenges of intervention not limited to UN peace operations. Some analysts see the main problem of such missions as maintaining domestic political support for an intervention. Bruce W. Jentleson and Rebecca Britton provide a thorough analysis of the impact public opinion has had on the use of American forces abroad, concluding that the "principal policy objective" more than any other variable determines the level of public support for an intervention.[17] Domestic support certainly matters, but it is not the only and sometimes not the most important variable determining success or failure of an intervention. Popular missions have failed and successful ones have been mounted with limited public support. Success depends on a broad range of factors that must be considered in order to derive a more effective approach to intervention.

Other studies consider the effectiveness of interventions. Jun Koga has discerned the tendency of democratic states to support threatened democracies.[18] James Meernik argues that interventions to promote democracy have generally not been effective.[19] Stephen Gent maintains that interventions in support of rebels have been more effective than interventions in support of threatened governments. He notes, however, that this divergence may be due to the timing of interventions. The United States generally supports rebels who are growing in strength but supports threatened governments only when they show signs of weakness. This delay may explain why intervention to support regimes threatened by insurgency have often failed.[20] Finally, Benjamin Fordham considers whether improved military capabilities increase the likelihood that a state will mount an intervention. While he notes some correlation between capability and the propensity to intervene, he also concludes that the increasing reliance of states on smaller professional armies equipped with a limited number of expensive, high-tech weapons mitigates this tendency.[21]

Another group of analysts focuses on the consequences of interventions. Jeffrey Pickering and Emizet F. Kisangani examine the social, economic and political impact of interventions. They find that supportive interventions in nondemocratic states tend to strengthen autocratic rulers, and that hostile interventions weaken economic development.[22] Patricia Sullivan considers the question of why powerful states lose small wars. She concludes that victory in such conflicts depends on two factors: capacity and resolve. While powerful states have great capacity, they often lack resolve because they fail to calculate the cost in blood and treasure of winning even a limited war and ultimately prove unwilling to pay it.

While each of these studies makes a valuable contribution to the literature of unconventional conflict, none takes a comprehensive approach to examining intervention as a U.S. strategic and policy issue. They do not present an analytical framework designed to produce guidance for policymakers and strategic planners seeking to decide where, when, and how to intervene. Such a framework requires consideration of a set of interrelated questions applied to case studies from the post-Cold War world, which presents a different set of security challenges than those faced in previous eras.

ANALYTICAL FRAMEWORK

For the purpose of this analysis, intervention is defined as direct application of military force by U.S. air and/or ground units, and the length of the intervention considered the time period in which such kinetic operations occur. The five American-led interventions since 1989 provide a useful set of cases from which relevant lessons may be derived. To be comprehensive, however, an investigation of this kind must also examine conflicts during the same period in which the United States considered intervening but decided not to do so. The 1994 Rwandan genocide and the 2011-12 Syrian civil war (at least to date) are such noninterventions. Taken together, these seven cases will be studied using an analytical framework based upon five broad questions. First, could the intervention have achieved its objective at an acceptable cost in blood and treasure in a reasonable amount of time? Second, what policy considerations impacted the decision to intervene or not to intervene? Third, how did the United States undertake the operation? — Did it act unilaterally or in concert with allies? Did it employ airpower alone or use a combination of air and ground forces? — Fourth, was the operation followed by an occupation or support mission requiring a sustained U.S. presence? Fifth, was there a viable exit strategy? — Did the United States have a workable plan for disengaging its forces once it completed the mission? These questions need to be considered not solely as individual queries but also as an integrated set of issues shaping U.S. policy and strategy. Applying this analytical framework to past conflicts should make it possible to derive lessons that can help guide future decisions on whether or not to intervene and improve the conduct of such interventions Washington chooses to undertake.

Somalia.

The Mission.

Altruism rarely guides foreign policy. States often use humanitarian intervention to mask self-interested motives. If ever there were an exception to this rule, however, the 1992 mission to Somalia is it. Having lost the 1992 election to Bill Clinton, President George H. W. Bush was free to act without consideration of his political career. No compelling foreign policy interest dictated intervention in the Horn of Africa, and Bush had no partisan incentive to become involved. Indeed, a careful look at conditions in the failed state dictated caution. In fact, he was advised not to get involved in the country's intractable civil war. In a biography of her father, Doro Bush Koch, maintains that Bush had watched images of starving Somalis for months until he "could bear it no more."[23] In his Memoir, President Bill Clinton acknowledges that the motives for going to Somalia were humanitarian as does Bush's Secretary of State James Baker.[24] Philosophically, President Bush also believed that the United States should play a leading role in what had been dubbed "the new world order." Flush from its victory in the Gulf War and having successfully mounted Operation PROVIDE COMFORT to protect the Kurds of northern Iraq, the U.S. military felt confident it could accomplish most missions in the post-Cold War world.

Somalia would put that confidence to the test. The country of nearly 8 million people was desperately poor, with 60 percent of its population engaged in agriculture, herding, or fishing.[25] Following the ouster of hated dictator Siyadd Barre in January 1991, Somalia dissolved into civil war, fracturing along clan and sub-clan lines. The chaos produced a massive humanitarian crisis. Between November 1991 and January 1992, 300,000 people died and another 4.5 million faced the prospect of severe malnutrition.[26] The humanitarian community poured aid into the war-torn country but found its efforts hampered by the conflict. Relief organizations and the Somali government, which controlled little more than a portion of the capital Mogadishu, asked for UN Assistance to protect delivery of food.

The UN eagerly responded. Like the United States, the international organization was experiencing a new-found confidence as the end of the Cold War broke the Security Council deadlock and made possible missions that would never have been approved a few years before. The Security Council approved the United Nations Operation in Somalia (UNOSOM I) to support the humanitarian effort. The mission initially called for 50 military observers but was soon expanded, first to 500 and then to 3500 troops. However, by December 1992, the UN had deployed only 564 personnel to Mogadishu and most of these troops remained confined to base amid the deteriorating security situation.[27] Failure of the warring parties to adhere to a ceasefire and the growing humanitarian crisis required a more robust intervention.

President Bush decided in late November to commit 25,000 U.S. troops as the core of a 37,000-strong Unified Task Force (UNITAF) deployed to bring some semblance of order to the chaos in Somalia. The troops secured the port and airport of Mogadishu and the ports of Baidoa and Kishmaayo. In a series of raids and firefights UNITAF achieved dominance in its area of operation and imposed conditions on the warring factions embodied in U.S. force commander Robert Johnston's four no's: "no technicals [pick-up trucks with crew-serviced weapons] . . .; no banditry; no road-blocks; no visible weapons."[28] As long as the armed groups obeyed these rules, he left them alone. In addition to a clear mandate and robust rules of engagement, success depended on cooperation between the numerous humanitarian organizations working within the country. A Civil-Military Cooperation Center (CMOC) in Mogadishu coordinated activities between the military and 49 nongovernmental organizations (NGOs).[29] Tensions between the Soldiers and the aid workers remained, but cooperation improved. Military leaders also met with Somali warlords on a regular basis. These meetings reduced the number of confrontations between the two and so lowered the level of violence in the capital. By April the famine had been alleviated, and UNITAF was prepared to hand over responsibility to a UN peacekeeping mission. Had the United States chosen to withdraw completely in May 1993, the UNITAF intervention would have been seen as a significant success.

Instead of declaring victory and going home, however, the United States agreed to contribute troops to an ill-conceived follow-on mission that proved disastrous. The UN Mission in Somalia II (UNOSOM II) operated under a broad and dangerously vague mandate that it lacked the means to implement. The enabling resolution that created the mission by augmenting UNOSOM I gave it a wider array of tasks, including safeguarding humanitarian aid, training national police, and promoting a stable government.

It also emphasized "the crucial importance of disarmament."[30] Secretary-General Boutros Boutros-Ghali interpreted this clause as a carte blanche to forcibly disarm any armed group that did not voluntarily surrender its weapons. This mandate insured that rather than being a Phase 4 stability operation, UNOSOM II would be an armed intervention in an active civil war.

The United States contributed a much smaller contingent to UNOSOM II — 3,000 support personnel and a rapid reaction force of 1,150 — not enough troops to make a difference but enough to get the United States embroiled in a crisis. Divided command increased this risk. Turkish General Çevik Bir commanded the UN Force, but the American troops remained under U.S. operational control. The rapid reaction force might be called upon to provide support in a crisis. This arrangement meant that the United States would have no control over the ill-advised policy of seizing weapons but might be called upon to recoup a deteriorating security situation. To make matters worse, U.S. forces in Somalia would not have all the assets, such as armor, they might need in a crisis and would have to ask for support from UNOSOM II.

Trying to enforce an expanded mandate with a weaker contingent soon led to disaster. On June 5, 1993, Somali fighters belonging to the Somali National Alliance led by warlord Mohammed Farrah Aidid ambushed Pakistani soldiers returning from a weapons search at the Mogadishu radio station. They killed 25 Pakistanis and wounded 57 others, including three Americans from the rapid reaction force deployed to rescue the UN contingent.[31] Violence escalated throughout the summer, and by the fall, the UN and the United States had decided to move against Aidid. This decision led to the infamous "Black Hawk

Down" incident. On October 3, 1993, U.S. Army Rangers and Delta Force Commandos came under attack as they returned from a raid on Aidid's headquarters that failed to capture the war lord. The ensuing rescue operation left 300 Somalis and 18 Americans dead, including the helicopter pilot whose body Somalis dragged through the streets of Mogadishu in front of TV cameras.[32] The U.S. command lacked the armor needed to rescue its Soldiers, and UNOSOM II did not provide it in a timely manner.

The October 3 incident marked the beginning of the end for UNOSOM II. The United States withdrew its forces by the end of the year, and the mission languished until it was withdrawn in March 1995. The UN intervention failed to accomplish any of its goals. In fact, its presence contributed to the loss of life, as some peacekeepers and many more Somalis died, particularly during the withdrawal, Operation UNITED SHIELD.

The Assessment.

Viewed as a single mission, the Somalia intervention failed. Despite alleviating famine, it did nothing to bring peace and stability to the country. Warring factions continue to battle for control of what has become the quintessential failed state. Interventions by Ethiopia, the African Union, and Kenya have failed to restore order throughout the country. Today Somalia hosts the al-Qaeda affiliate al-Shabab, a source of regional instability and international terrorism. For purposes of analysis, however, it makes sense to consider UNITAF and UNOSOM II as two separate enforcement operations. Considered in light of the five questions posed by this examination, the

American-led mission comes off much better than its UN successor.

As already noted, the Bush White House intervened in Somalia for altruistic reasons rather than out of strategic self-interest. The intervention had a reasonable chance to alleviate the famine. Operation RESTORE HOPE (the U.S. name for the UNITAF mission) adopted a highly focused, eminently achievable goal: safeguarding delivery of humanitarian aid. American forces secured ports, cleared armed groups from the streets of Mogadishu, and protected humanitarian organizations. They assiduously refused to take sides in the internecine struggle despite pressure from UN Secretary-General Boutros Boutros-Ghali to do so. The means employed suited the ends. The UN-approved UNITAF and participation by a coalition of nations gave it greater legitimacy than it would have enjoyed as a purely U.S. operation. The coalition deployed sufficient forces to achieve the limited objective. American troops operated under robust rules of engagement but applied them in a clear, focused manner. American forces used all available means to protect aid shipments but did not become a player in the civil war. The intervention did require a follow-on stability mission but had a clear exit strategy. Conceived as a short-term humanitarian mission, UNITAF planned to hand-over operations to the UN within 6 months. The Bush administration and the military command thus appear to have considered carefully all the questions posed by this analysis.

By comparison, U.S. participation in UNISOM II failed because it deviated from the approach taken by its predecessor. It was a badly conceived UN enforcement operation whose goals could not be achieved at a cost in blood and treasure acceptable to the troop-contributing nations, especially the United States. The American role in the mission was ambiguous from the start and escalated as events unfolded. While UNITAF aimed at the limited objective of safeguarding humanitarian aid, UNISOM II took on the much more ambitious task of disarming the warring factions and ending the civil war, yet tried to do so with a smaller, more polyglot force than UNITAF deployed. When it moved against Aidid, the mission became a participant in the civil war. It also lacked the means to achieve its objective. UNITAF had a hard core of 20,000 well-equipped U.S. troops while UNOSOM II's largest element was a Pakistani contingent of 4,973.[33] Beyond disarming the warring factions and forcibly ending hostilities, the UN had no precise plan for rebuilding the country and no clear exit strategy. Even without the disastrous October 3 incident, it is hard to imagine how the intervention could have ended well.

Haiti.

The Mission.

Few Latin American states have had such a turbulent and tragic history as the tiny Caribbean nation of Haiti. Crowded into an area slightly smaller than the state of Maryland, most of the country's 9.8 million people live in poverty as their ancestors have done for at least the past century.[34] They have lived under a series of dictators whose oppressive rule has been punctuated by natural disasters and American occupations. Since gaining independence in 1804, Haiti has had 21 constitutions and 41 heads of state, 29 of whom were deposed or assassinated.[35] The 1994 mission was the latest in a long series of U.S. interventions, but it occurred under different circumstances than previous operations. The end of the Cold War made it possible for the United States to participate in UN peacekeeping missions, but the debacle of Somalia had soured the American public on humanitarian intervention.

Besides a desire to relieve Haitian suffering, however, self-interest motivated the United States to intervene in Haiti. Lieutenant General Raoul Cédras, Chief of the Haitian Armed Forces, had staged a coup that toppled President Jean Baptiste Aristide and unleashed a reign of terror against the president's supporters. In the ensuing chaos, 40,000 Haitians fled abroad, many of them arriving as illegal immigrants on the shores of Florida.[36] The refugee crisis made the Haitian problem an American one.

President Bush responded by deporting refugees back to Haiti, a policy for which his challenger in the 1992 presidential election Bill Clinton and human rights groups took him to task. Once in office, though, Clinton continued the practice in the face of equally vociferous protest. The only other option seemed to be regime change in Haiti. Before invading the country, however, Clinton tried to find a diplomatic solution to the Haitian crisis. His administration brokered the Governor's Island Agreement signed on July 3, 1993. Under the terms of the agreement, the Haitian military had promised to restore democracy, but when Haitian mobs prevented the USS *Harlan County*, with its small multinational peacekeeping force sent to implement the Agreement, from docking at Port au Prince, it became clear that the junta would not go quietly. "By this time," Clinton wrote in his memoirs, "I had been working for a peaceful solution for 2 years, and I was fed up."[37]

Washington pursued a two-track strategy to resolve the Haitian crisis. As it prepared to invade Haiti, the Clinton administration continued to work towards a diplomatic solution that would remove Cédras and allow a permissive entry of U.S. forces into the island nation. The Pentagon tasked different units to prepare for each scenario. The 82nd Airborne Division geared up for an invasion while the 10th Mountain Division planned for a permissive entry. The threat of force, Clinton hoped, might be enough to convince Cédras to relinquish power voluntarily. To make that threat more credible and garner international support for the mission, the United States sought UN approval for intervening in Haiti. The Security Council called upon member states to form a coalition, acting under Chapter 7 of the UN Charter:

- to use all necessary means to facilitate the departure from Haiti of the military,
- to provide leadership consistent with the Governors Island Agreement,
- to facilitate the prompt return of the legitimately elected President and the restoration of the legitimate authorities of the Government of Haiti,
- and to establish and maintain a secure and stable environment that will permit implementation of the Governors Island Agreement on the understanding that the cost of implementing this temporary operation will be borne by the participating Member States.[38]

With a strong UN mandate and troops prepared to deploy, the United States had an unbeatable diplomatic hand. On September 18, 1994, a delegation led by former President Jimmy Carter and retired General

Colin Powell persuaded General Cédras to leave the island and allow the Multinational Force (MNF) (consisting almost entirely of U.S. troops) to enter Haiti. Units of the 10th Mountain Division began deploying as soon as the dictator left until a force of over 20,000 occupied Haiti.[39] The troops disembarked without losing a single Soldier.

The mission itself went reasonably well. Contrary to optimistic expectations, the civil police did not continue to function after the collapse of the junta. U.S. troops were forced into a policing role for which they were ill prepared. Initial rules of engagement (ROEs) did not allow them use of deadly force even to stop murders committed before their eyes. Lawless elements exploited this vacuum (a lesson apparently lost on the planners of Operation IRAQI FREEDOM), but once the ROEs were adjusted, the situation improved dramatically. Besides suppressing lawlessness, troops secured the port, the capital, and other strategic points and patrolled the countryside. They disarmed and disbanded the Haitian Army and paramilitaries. On March 31, 1995, U.S. forces handed over responsibility for stability operations to the UN Mission in Haiti (UNMIH) and withdrew the bulk of their troops.

The Assessment.

By almost any measure, the U.S. intervention in Haiti succeeded. It fulfilled every objective detailed in the UN mandate, at least in the short run. General Cédras left the country, and President Aristide returned. American troops provided security so that the follow-on UN mission could work to rebuild the police force and ensure that elections would take place. Improved conditions stemmed the flow of refugees into south Florida. Long-term stability, which could only be based upon economic development and social change, has proven more elusive, but the U.S. mission can hardly be blamed for that problem. The analytical questions discussed here provide a framework for explaining why the intervention succeeded.

To begin with, the intervention had a focused, achievable goal. Although the Clinton administration did wish to alleviate the suffering of the Haitian people, it aimed first and foremost to stop Haitian refugees entering the United States. Restoring Democracy was a means to that end, not an end in itself. Without the refugee crisis, Washington would probably not have intervened merely to remove a dictator, especially with the memory of Somalia still so fresh. It had been more than willing to work with Latin American tyrants throughout the 20th century.

The means chosen to achieve the mission also contributed to its success. The United States had long considered the Caribbean its backyard and could easily have intervened unilaterally in Haiti as it had done in the past. A multilateral approach, however, gave the mission greater international legitimacy and perhaps made it more palatable to an American public soured on humanitarian intervention.[40] As Sarah Kreps has demonstrated, however, Operation UPHOLD DEMOCRACY was multilateral in name only. All the planning and virtually all of the combat troops deployed were American. The United States thus enjoyed the legitimacy conveyed by multilateralism with few of its constraints.[41] Under such circumstances coercive diplomacy backed by the threat of overwhelming military force made permissive entry of U.S. forces into Haiti possible.

In addition to an achievable objective and appropriate means for achieving it, Operation UPHOLD DEMOCRACY had a viable exit strategy. Washington knew from the outset that its occupation of Haiti would be short term and that it would hand over to a UN mission. UNMIH had actually been created in September 1993, but the junta had prevented peacekeepers from deploying, thus necessitating the threat of a more robust American operation. In January 1995 the Security Council extended UNMIH's mandate for another 6 months, allowing it to take over from the MNF on March 31. The Security Council determined "that a secure and stable environment, appropriate to the deployment of UNMIH as foreseen in the above-mentioned resolution 940 (1994), now exists in Haiti," and that the mission could commence rebuilding the army and police.[42] The United States contributed a much smaller contingent to this truly multinational mission.

Having learned from its mistakes in Somalia, the Clinton administration considered all the relevant issues before it intervened in Haiti. Fortunately, the threat of force eliminated any need to actually use it. U.S. troops conducted a short, decisive operation to achieve a reasonable goal. The mission enjoyed international legitimacy without the constraints imposed by alliance or coalition politics. The U.S. contingent suffered virtually no casualties, and the last Soldier came home before any domestic opposition to the operation could even begin to form.

Bosnia.

The Mission.

The United States never wished to become involved in what analysts now call the wars of Yugoslav succession. Neither President George H. W. Bush nor his successor, Bill Clinton, saw any compelling reason to intervene in a violent ethnic conflict taking place in an area with no strategic resources or compelling U.S. interests. "We don't have a dog in this fight," remarked Bush's Secretary of Defense James Baker.[43] Since NATO's European members proclaimed their readiness to go it alone in dealing with Europe's first post-Cold War crisis, and the UN proved willing to sanction a large peace operation in the Balkans, the United States had no reason to intervene.

Neither NATO rhetoric nor UN resolutions, however, could overcome Serbia's military advantage. Once Slovenia successfully seceded in June 1991, Croatia and Bosnia soon followed, triggering a grab for territory. As it controlled most of the Yugoslav military, Serbia had the upper hand. Its forces over-ran the Serb-populated Krajina region and Eastern Slavonia, both part of Croatia. Serbia then transferred control of its military material in Bosnia to the province's Serb units. Paramilitaries from Serbia proper began a brutal campaign of ethnic cleansing using rape and murder to force Croats and Bosnian Muslims from their homes.

The international community responded to the escalating violence with halting, largely ineffective steps. In September 1991, the UN imposed an arms embargo on the belligerents.[44] Then in February 1992, the Security Council created the UN Protection Force

(UNPROFOR) to monitor the ceasefire in Croatia, to supervise protected areas, and to secure implementation of a peace plan worked out by UN Representative Cyrus Vance.[45] Before UNPROFOR even fully deployed, however, fighting spread to Bosnia-Herzegovina, a patchwork quilt of Serb, Croat, and Muslim communities with a Muslim plurality. With their preponderance in arms, Bosnian Serb units occupied much of the newly independent country and continued their brutal policy of ethnic cleansing. At first, Bosnian Croats and Muslims allied to defend themselves against the Serbs but then fell to fighting each other in a grab for territory once partition of Bosnia seemed likely. The lightly-armed peacekeeping force that eventually numbered 30,000 could do little to stop the bloodshed and barely managed to protect Muslim enclaves dubbed "safe areas" with the help of NATO aircraft.

As violence continued throughout the next 2 years, the balance of forces slowly shifted against the Bosnian Serbs. With the help of a private military company based in the United States, the Croats rebuilt their small army into a formidable fighting force. Impatient with Bosnian Serb violations of various ceasefires and exacerbated with the failure of UNPROFOR to prevent them, NATO deployed a more robust Rapid Reaction Force on Mount Igman above the Bosnian capital Sarajevo. The UN, however, remained reluctant to sanction an enforcement operation, barring further provocation from the Serbs. That provocation came in July 1995 at the UN-declared "safe area" of Srebrenica. Bosnian government forces had used the safe area as an enclave from which to raid surrounding Serb territory, but withdrew as Serb forces closed in. The withdrawal of Bosnian troops did not, however, stop

Bosnian Serb units under General Radko Mladic from perpetrating the worst massacre of civilians in Europe since the end of World War II. Between July 11 and 22, Serb forces murdered 7-8,000 men and boys, the vast majority of them unarmed civilians.[46]

The UN and NATO now faced an inescapable choice: withdraw UNPROFOR or mount a more robust military action to stop the genocide. A July 17 internal memo from NATO headquarters in Zagreb, Croatia discussed these options in detail. Withdrawing more than 40,000 troops from an active war zone would be both difficult and humiliating for the NATO alliance engaged in its first real combat mission. The memo considered that forcing open the road to Sarajevo should be the immediate course of action, although it had to admit that doing so would do nothing to help the other besieged safe areas.[47] Four days later, the Contact Group of six nations formed to deal with the Bosnian crisis gave NATO power to authorize airstrikes without UN approval.[48] The allies then delivered an ultimatum to Belgrade, warning that it would conduct airstrikes against Bosnian Serb units should any more attacks on safe areas occur.[49]

During the ensuing month, several developments tilted the balance decisively against Bosnian Serb forces. On August 4, the revamped Croat Army launched Operation STORM and recaptured the Krajina. Director of Peacekeeping Operations (later Secretary-General) Kofi Annan ordered UNPROFOR to "intensify measures already underway to regroup all personnel in vulnerable positions" so that they could not be taken hostage as had occurred earlier in the year.[50] Meanwhile the United States had become heavily engaged in efforts to end the Bosnian conflict, pressuring the government of Serbia to end its support for the Bosnian Serbs and committing military resources to an enforcement operation, should that become necessary.

The long-expected provocation necessary for a stronger NATO response came on August 28, when a mortar shell landed in the Sarajevo marketplace killing 37 people. Although Bosnian Serb forces (and some analysts) insisted that they had not fired at the city that day, few at the time believed them. Early on the morning of August 30, NATO aircraft began systematic bombing of Serb Army positions while the guns of the Rapid Reaction Force lifted the siege of Sarajevo. A month of bombing ensued during which Bosnian government forces advanced eastward from the Bihac pocket in northeastern Bosnia. On October 6, 1995, the Bosnian Serbs accepted a dictated ceasefire. In December, the Dayton Peace Accords ended the war, effectively partitioning Bosnia and mandating the presence of an International Force (IFOR) of 60,000 NATO and partner nation troops to implement the agreement. Although it would take another decade for the United States to disengage from Bosnia, the stabilization missions that followed the Dayton Peace Accords did not involve kinetic operations. Not a single American Soldier, Sailor, Airman, or Marine died from hostile action during the post-conflict stabilization missions.

Assessment.

Armed intervention in Bosnia-Herzegovina, belated though it was, achieved its objectives of stopping the genocide and imposing a peace accord on the warring factions. Stabilization of the country would take much longer, but the phase of kinetic operations by U.S. forces was very brief. The United States provided most of the NATO airpower for the bombing campaign and contributed the largest contingent of troops to IFOR. The mission suffered no combat casualties, though one soldier died in an explosion, and thus provoked no serious opposition at home. IFOR kept the peace, transitioned to a smaller Stabilization Force (SFOR) in 1996, and handed over to a European Force (EUFOR) in 2004. Again, the analytical questions herein provide a useful framework for assessing the mission.

By August 1995 a U.S. intervention to support NATO, with the limited objective of ending the war, could be achieved at acceptable cost. During the previous 3 years, the United States had determined that intervention would require too large a commitment and carry with it too many risks. NATO estimated that ending the war and reversing Serb advances would have required a combat force of 150,000-460,000 troops, half of them Americans.[51] The force would have had to engage Bosnian Serb units and would almost certainly have suffered casualties. After the Somalia debacle, the Clinton administration was understandably reluctant to participate in such a mission.

By the summer of 1995, however, circumstances had changed so dramatically that a much smaller commitment of resources could be expected to achieve a desired end state at reasonable cost with acceptable risk. The policy debate had also shifted. The United States still had no overwhelming strategic interest in Bosnia per se, but it did have a strong desire to see NATO continue as a viable military alliance. Preventing that alliance from failing in its first out of area operation may thus have been a consideration in Washington. Stung by criticism of its failure to stop the Rwandan genocide, the Clinton administration may also have felt a moral obligation to stop genocide in the Balkans. To avoid a repeat of Somalia, however, the United States stuck to the narrowest definition of its mission, enforcing the partition plan of the Dayton Accords but refusing to implement its more problematic goals, such as pursuing indicted war criminals.

The means the Clinton administration employed to conduct the intervention contributed to its success. The United States intervened as part of the NATO mission Operation DELIBERATE FORCE, with the approval of the UN. The United States led the air campaign, while the Rapid Reaction Force used its artillery to lift the siege of Sarajevo, and Bosnian forces advanced out of the Bihac pocket in northwest Bosnia. American warplanes conducted the bulk of the air attacks, flying 2,318 (65 percent) of 3,515 sorties.[52] Use of airpower had significant advantages. Overwhelming air superiority meant that U.S. forces risked few, if any, casualties during the operation. Low risk of loss and the short duration of the operation reduced the likelihood of domestic opposition to the intervention.

NATO linked Operation DELIBERATE FORCE to a diplomatic effort designed to end the conflict and allow permissive entry of a follow-on stabilization mission. The air campaign aimed not only to check Bosnian Serb advances against the safe areas, but to force the political leadership in Serbia proper to the bargaining table. The Dayton Accords signed in December 1995 effectively partitioned Bosnia-Herzegovina, while forcing the belligerents into a reluctant federation. The U.S. military contributed 24,000 troops and 12,000 pieces of major equipment to Operation JOINT ENDEAVOR, its contingent in IFOR, which consisted of approximately 60,000 NATO personnel.[53]

Such a large deployment, of course, carried the risk of American casualties. The Clinton administration took two steps to reduce that risk: it imposed rigorous force protection guidelines on all American units, and defined the mission very narrowly. U.S. troops operated from within heavily defended bases from which they ventured forth in full "battle rattle," creating the absurd situation of Americans in helmets and flak jackets watching other contingents jog past their camp in shorts and t-shirts. U.S. Forces also stuck to the narrowest interpretation of their mission. The Dayton Accords gave IFOR the right to:

    a. monitor and help ensure compliance by all parties with this Annex (including, in particular, withdrawal and redeployment of Forces within agreed periods, and the establishment of Zones of Separation);

    b. authorize and supervise the selective marking of the Agreed Cease-Fire Line and its Zone of Separation and the Inter-Entity Boundary Line and its Zone of Separation as established by the General Framework Agreement;

    c. establish liaison arrangements with local civilian and military authorities and other international organizations as necessary for the accomplishment of its mission; and,

    d. assist in the withdrawal of UN Peace Forces not transferred to the IFOR, including, if necessary, the emergency withdrawal of UNCRO [United Nations Confidence Restoration Operation based in Croatia] Forces.[54]

The Accords also committed IFOR to assist humanitarian organizations and, some believed, required troop contributors to apprehend war criminals. The U.S. contingent refused to engage in this latter task for fear that it would bring them into violent conflict with Bosnian Serb forces. Thus by taking no unnecessary chances, the Clinton administration kept the risk of casualties low.

As Washington found once again, however, getting out of a country is much more difficult than getting in to it. The Dayton Peace Accords ended the conflict, but everyone realized that they would have to be implemented by a substantial military force. In his memoirs, President Clinton acknowledges that the American public still opposed sending ground troops to Bosnia, and the Pentagon was ambivalent about the prospect.[55] Even the President's allies in Congress lent their support only on the condition that the mission had a viable exit strategy.[56]

Whatever he may have promised at the time, the U.S. deployment lasted longer than Clinton intended. In December 1996, IFOR was replaced by SFOR with about half the number of U.S. troops. This troop reduction did not, however, mollify critics who claimed that the administration still had no exit strategy for its Bosnia mission. The following year, a *New York Times* editorial criticized Clinton for what was looking more and more like an open-ended commitment. "Everyone wants a unified, democratic and prospering Bosnia," the opinion piece concluded. "But Congressional Republicans are right to warn that American Soldiers cannot remain deployed until that goal is fully achieved."[57] It would take another 8 years before SFOR handed over to EUFOR, and the United States withdrew all but a small contingent from Bosnia.

Criticism over lack of an exit strategy does not, however, seem to have hampered President Clinton's ability to conduct the Bosnia mission, perhaps because it never escalated to a popular out-cry to bring the troops home. Clinton claimed that the real problem the deployment posed had to do with justifying its expense to Congress.[58] Complete absence of combat operations, let alone casualties, may explain why the mission produced no serious opposition at home during the 8 years American troops deployed to Bosnia. In the 2000 presidential election, then-Governor George W. Bush campaigned against using U.S forces for nation-building, but once in office he did not withdraw the U.S. contingents from Bosnia or Kosovo.

The U.S. intervention in Bosnia clearly achieved its goals, however modest those goals may have been. Along with its NATO allies, U.S. forces stopped the genocide, imposed a peace settlement, and stabilized Bosnia-Herzegovina through disarmament, demining, humanitarian assistance, and policing. Tragically, conditions for a successful intervention may have existed as early as 1992, and had such an intervention occurred then, it would have saved tens of thousands of lives. That sad fact does not, however, diminish the success of the 1995 mission. Today the Bosnian Federation remains a peaceful but fragile state in continuing need of foreign aid, but the chances of renewed conflict in the foreseeable future remain low.

The ability of the Clinton administration to provide satisfactory answers to only four of the five analytical questions posed by this Paper reveals a great deal about the conditions necessary for successful intervention. Despite the emphasis of policymakers and strategists on the need to have a clear exit strategy before mounting an intervention, the Bosnian case demonstrates that the absence of such a strategy does not preclude an intervention or consign it to failure. Critics chided the President for not stating how and when he planned to withdraw from IFOR/SFOR, but such criticism never reached a level high enough to affect policy. Compared with the Somalia debacle, the Bosnian mission suggests that lack of an exit strategy only becomes a serious problem when combined with rising casualties.

Kosovo.

The Mission.

The Kosovo conflict was the last of the wars of Yugoslav succession. Ironically, the chain of events that led to these wars began and ended in Kosovo. The southern province of Serbia, with its Muslim majority, had enjoyed autonomy in Tito's Yugoslavia. In 1989, however, during the 600th anniversary of the Battle of Kosovo Polje, in which Serbian Prince Lazar died fighting the Turks, Yugoslav President Slobodan Milošević revoked that autonomy. Milošević persecuted Kosovo's two million Albanians (86 percent of its population) while privileging a Serbian minority (10 percent of the population).[59] For the next decade, Kosovars suffered systematic discrimination in all areas of economic and social life.

With no resources and little outside support, the Kosovars could not challenge the vastly superior Serbian-dominated Yugoslav security forces. They opted instead for passive resistance, creating a parallel "state" that provided basic education, health care, and even a sports program to meet the needs of their people, while biding their time until their political fortunes improved.[60] The situation in Kosovo changed dramatically in 1997. The government of neighboring Albania collapsed, losing control of some of its weapons depots. A radical fringe group, the Kosovo Liberation Army (KLA), exploited the situation by importing guns across the largely open border with Albania and launching an insurgency against the Serbian government. They adopted a classic guerrilla strategy, attacking police and government officials to provoke the security forces into over-reacting. They

hoped this approach might draw international attention to their cause. The strategy worked brilliantly.[61]
In the fall of 1997, Belgrade sent in regular army units
to clear the central Drenica region of insurgents. The
troops killed 136 people, including 11 children and 23
women, and sparked an exodus of 250,000 Kosovar
Albanians.[62] The violence continued throughout 1998,
and all efforts to reach a diplomatic solution failed. On
March 23, 1999, the United States led a 78-day bombing campaign that forced Serbia to withdraw its forces
from Kosovo.

A NATO peacekeeping mission numbering close
to 50,000 troops dubbed "Kosovo Force" (KFOR)
deployed to help implement the peace agreement and
rebuild the war-torn province. That force, albeit much
reduced in number, remains to this day providing
security to Kosovo, which declared its independence
in February 2008. Despite the seemingly open-ended
nature of the U.S. commitment to the tiny country,
criticism of the mission never reached the levels it had
with Bosnia, although George W. Bush campaigned on
a promise to avoid future nation-building missions. A
number of factors explain the absence of any serious
demand to bring the troops home. To begin with, the
United States contributed far fewer Soldiers to KFOR
than it had to IFOR. Task Force Falcon consisted of just
8,453 troops occupying one of the quietest sectors in
the province.[63] Their numbers steadily declined to the
current strength of 781.[64] As with the Bosnia mission,
troops engaged in no combat operations and suffered
no casualties from violence. A 2003 Rand Corporation Report described the Kosovo intervention as "the
best managed of the U.S. post–Cold War ventures in
nation-building."[65] More than anything else, however,
the September 11, 2001 (9/11) attacks followed by the

invasions of Afghanistan and Iraq almost completely eclipsed the small operation in the Balkans.

Analysis.

The Kosovo intervention proved highly successful. A large-scale NATO/UN mission followed the air campaign and stabilized Kosovo, creating a safe environment for a massive humanitarian aid effort. Albanian refugees returned en-mass, but most Serbians and Roma (Gypsies), fearful of reprisals, did not. Efforts to reintegrate Kosovo as an autonomous province of Serbia failed. On February 17, 2008, Kosovo declared independence. The United States and most of its NATO allies have recognized the new country, while Russia, China, and, of course, Serbia have not. A token military presence backed up by the might of the NATO alliance guarantees Kosovo's security, but the tiny state remains dependent upon foreign aid. The success of the mission may be explained by considering the analytical questions of this Paper.

The U.S.-led intervention succeeded largely because its goals were achievable. Neither the United States nor its NATO allies sought to create an independent Kosovo. They aimed first and foremost to stop the ethnic cleansing (expulsion of non-Serbians) and prevent the regional destabilization the refugee crisis threatened to cause. Hoping that the province could be reintegrated with Serbia, NATO forces worked to assist return of Serbian refugees, and only reluctantly supported the province's independence. Intervention carried little risk of escalation as Russia, Serbia's historic protector, showed no strong inclination to back it over Kosovo and even encouraged Serbian President Slobodan Milošević to come to terms with

NATO. Russian forces briefly occupied the Pristina airport, but that episode had more to do with Russian domestic politics and a demand for inclusion in the follow-on mission than with trying to prevent it from taking place.[66] In any event, the willingness of NATO member Hungary and NATO aspirants Romania and Bulgaria to close their airspace to Russian aircraft precluded further action by Moscow.

The formulation of U.S. policy towards Kosovo evolved over time, but the goals of that policy remained consistent. The United States did not want a Kosovar refugee crisis destabilizing the surrounding states, and to that end, it favored restoration of the province's autonomy.[67] Although it had no desire to go to war over Kosovo, Washington had remained committed to curbing Serbian excesses in the province since it first threatened use of force to stop them. On December 25, 1992, President George H. W. Bush had sent the "Christmas warning" to Yugoslav President Slobodan Milošević: "In the event of conflict in Kosovo caused by Serbian action, the United States will be prepared to employ military force against the Serbians in Kosovo and in Serbia proper."[68] The Clinton administration took the same position, reiterating Bush's warning in February 1993 and June 1998, as the crisis in the province worsened. "I am determined to do all I can to stop a repeat of the human carnage in Bosnia and the 'ethnic cleansing'," Clinton declared. "And I have authorized, and I am supporting, an accelerated planning process for NATO."[69] Despite its willingness to use force, however, the White House sought a diplomatic solution via the Rambouillet Peace Conference. Only when that peace process failed, did the United States lead the alliance into war.

The means by which the United States conducted the Kosovo intervention also evolved. Alliances often produce least-common-denominator strategy, with the most reluctant members setting the pace of operations. In this case, the United States was one of the reluctant members of NATO. Although the UN condemned Serbian atrocities against Kosovar Albanians, it imposed a (largely meaningless) arms embargo on Yugoslavia (now reduced to Serbia and Montenegro) and threatened further measures if the Milošević regime did not comply with its demands. The Security Council fell short of approving armed intervention because of a threatened Russian veto. Believing that it had a strong moral argument and considerable international support and calculating that Russia could do little more than protest, the Clinton administration decided to lead NATO into its first war against a sovereign state. Stung by the experience of Somalia, however, the White House joined those allies opposed to a ground invasion. The United Kingdom (UK) unconditionally favored use of ground troops, France supported their use with UN approval, and Italy and Germany opposed ground action entirely.[70]

Under the circumstances, an air campaign, which most analysts believed would be short and decisive, seemed the best option. In his address to the nation at the start of hostilities, however, the President made a statement that reduced the likelihood that the bombing would promptly resolve the situation. By announcing that air strikes would be directed at Serb forces in Kosovo and declaring emphatically that he did not "intend to put our troops in Kosovo to fight a war," he essentially told the Serbs that they could disperse their tanks and other equipment, making it harder to destroy them from the air.[71] The tentative nature of military action encouraged Milošević to believe that NATO would not remain unified enough to sustain a long air war. He might have been right were it not for another line in Clinton's speech, which he apparently missed. "Imagine what would happen if we and our allies instead decided just to look the other way, as these people were massacred on NATO's doorstep," the President asserted. "That would discredit NATO, the cornerstone on which our security has rested for 50 years now."[72] The credibility of NATO and perhaps even its survival were at stake. This realization strengthened, rather than weakened, the resolve of the alliance.

As the campaign unfolded, NATO increased its pressure on Serbia. When bombing targets in Kosovo failed to produce results, the alliance attacked Serbia proper. Although the allies disagreed on target selection during the initial phase of operations, by the time of the NATO Summit in April, they had become more focused in their objectives and unified in their effort.[73] Once again, the United States provided most of the assets for the air campaign, flying 5,035 strike sorties, 53 percent of the total.[74] All the states surrounding Serbia were either NATO members or aspired to membership, and so they cooperated in isolating Milošević. By June 1999, the alliance had built up ground forces on the Albanian and Macedonian borders and was discussing an invasion. With American help, the KLA had developed its capabilities to the point where the Serbian army had to concentrate troops and equipment to combat the insurgents, thus making its units vulnerable to air attack. This threat, coupled with Moscow pressuring him to give up, probably led Milošević to capitulate on June 9.[75] The 78-day NATO war was thus an example of effective coercive diplomacy in which military action, combined with diplomatic pressure, forced the Serbian president to withdraw his forces from Kosovo, allowing permissive entry of KFOR into the province.[76]

The NATO air campaign thus paved the way for a follow-on mission to provide security, deliver humanitarian aid, and rebuild civil institutions. Because of the bad experience they had in Bosnia, NATO forces did not wish to be under direct UN control, so the Security Council approved a dual mission. Resolution 1244 authorized "Member States and relevant international organizations to establish the international security presence in Kosovo."[77] That authorization allowed NATO to deploy KFOR, comprised of close to 50,000 troops derived primarily from member countries augmented by Partnership for Peace nations, including the Russian Federation.[78] The same resolution created the UN Mission in Kosovo (UNMIK) to handle the civil and political side of the intervention.

The United States managed its military commitment to KFOR very tightly. The 8,453-strong U.S. contingent operated under robust rules of engagement and stringent force protection guidelines that virtually eliminated the threat of casualties from hostile action.[79] While the White House remained committed to staying in Kosovo for an extended period of time, it planned to reduce its troop strength to a bare minimum as soon as possible. The 781 troops currently deployed to the mission represent a symbolic commitment to defending Kosovo's independence, a confidence-building measure that represents no serious drain on American military resources.[80]

The U.S.-led intervention accomplished its goal of stopping Serbian aggression against Kosovar Albanians, preventing the refugee crisis from destabilizing the region, and assuring the continued viability and relevance of NATO. Clinton's announcement that no ground troops would invade Kosovo hampered the air campaign, which took much longer than anticipated to achieve results. Thousands of Kosovars suffered and died as a result. The Clinton administration may, however, have mounted the only mission that the U.S. Congress and the American public would tolerate. It certainly accomplished its objective with minimal loss of U.S. lives and at an acceptable cost.

As was the case with the Bosnia crisis, the United States did not have a clear exit strategy, but lack of one did not hamper operations. It might also be argued that the military means used to mount the intervention did not produce the best result in the timeliest manner. Taking the threat of ground action off the table allowed the Serbs to disperse their forces, making them harder to destroy. The additional time needed to force Milošević to surrender resulted in considerable suffering among the very people the United States wished to help. However, the Clinton administration believed that a limited air campaign was the least-common-denominator strategy that the NATO alliance would support, and it did ultimately work. Whether the means employed will have been deemed appropriate depends on the outcome of the mission, which cannot be foreseen at the outset. Policymakers have little choice but to achieve a compromise between the most desirable and the best available means to intervene and hope for the best.

Libya.

The Mission.

The civil war that eventually drew in the United States and its NATO allies began on February 15, 2011, with an uprising in the eastern city of Benghazi. Inspired by the Arab Spring, which had toppled totalitarian regimes in Tunisia and Egypt, the rebels sought to remove Muammar Qaddafi from power. Although they enjoyed some early victories, the poorly trained and very disunified opposition faltered before Libya's regular armed forces. Qaddafi unleashed a reign of terror, attacking civilians as well as rebel fighters.

Led by France, Britain, and the United States, a coalition of nations sought to halt the violence. After the Arab League and the Secretary General of the Organization of the Islamic Conference condemned attacks upon civilians in Libya, the UN Security Council took up the matter. Resolution 1970 deplored "the gross and systematic violation of human rights, including the repression of peaceful demonstrators," expressed "deep concern at the deaths of civilians," and rejected "unequivocally the incitement to hostility and violence against the civilian population made from the highest level of the Libyan government."[81] The resolution imposed an arms embargo and travel ban on the country and froze Qaddafi's assets abroad.

Economic and diplomatic pressure had no effect on the dictator, who stepped up his attacks using aircraft to bomb rebel held towns and cities. In response the Security Council sanctioned limited military action to protect civilians. Resolution 1973 imposed a no-fly zone over Libya and authorized:

Member States that have notified the Secretary-General, acting nationally or through regional organizations or arrangements, and acting in cooperation with the Secretary-General, to take all necessary measures, notwithstanding paragraph 9 of resolution 1970 (2011), to protect civilians and civilian populated areas under threat of attack in the Libyan Arab Jamahiriya, including Benghazi, while excluding a foreign occupation force of any form on any part of Libyan territory.[82]

The resolution used language sufficiently ambiguous to allow different interpretations. Believing that it authorized little more than a no-fly zone over eastern Libya, Russia and China allowed the motion to pass by abstaining. "We believe that the interference of the coalition into the internal, civil war in Libya has not been sanctioned by the U.N. Security Council resolution," Russian Federation Foreign Minister Sergei Lavrov later declared.[83] The United States, France, Italy, and the UK, however, interpreted the phrase "all necessary measures" broadly. They moved beyond enforcing a no-fly zone to striking at government forces and installations, supplied the rebels with arms (UK and France), and even inserted covert operatives to gather intelligence (the U.S. Central Intelligence Agency [CIA]).

The air campaign lasted approximately 6 months. From March 19-31, the United States led Operation ODYSSEY DAWN, after which NATO took over command and continued the campaign until October 20. Although more than 18 nations contributed military assets to the mission, four conducted most of the attacks: the United States (2,000), Great Britain (1,300), France (1,200), and Italy (600).[84] The air campaign combined with aid to the rebels achieved decisive results without the loss of a single NATO soldier, sailor, or airman. By the end of August, the rebels controlled Tripoli, and the last regime stronghold of Sirte fell on October 20. During the final days of the campaign, rebel fighters found and summarily executed Muammar Qaddafi.

Analysis.

The Libyan intervention achieved the immediate goal of helping the rebels to overthrow Qaddafi. Since the United States did not participate in a Phase 4 stability operation, it incurred none of the costs and faced none of the criticisms common to the Somalia and Balkan missions. Whether the intervention will be deemed effective depends on how events play out in Libya. If an anti-Western Islamist government gains power, many will question the wisdom of backing the rebels. If the new regime enjoys good relations with Washington, London, and Paris, then few will question President Obama's decision to get involved. So far the signs from Tripoli have been mixed. Fair and free elections have taken place, Libyan oil is flowing again, and Western engagement is helping to rebuild the country. The murder of the U.S. Ambassador in Benghazi in September 2012, however, reveals the fragile state of the country. As of this writing, the new government is barely 1 year old, so it is far too early to tell how things will turn out. Russia's determination to block intervention in Syria must, however, be considered an unintended negative consequence of the Libyan mission. The Libyan intervention can be assessed by answering analytical questions posed by this analysis.

The question of whether or not the intervention could achieve its goal seems clear in retrospect, but it was not so clear at the outset of the operation. However, Gent's conclusion that supporting rebels who are gaining strength usually succeeds suggests that the administration was backing the winning horse.[85] As commentators noted at the time, imposing a no-fly zone would require offensive military action. Besides violating the airspace of a sovereign state, it requires destroying that state's air defense system (aircraft, missiles, radar installations, etc.). "Let's just call a spade a spade," Secretary of Defense Robert Gates told Congress. "A no-fly zone begins with an attack on Libya to destroy the air defenses."[86] Although the United States and its allies could easily impose a no-fly zone, whether doing so would actually protect civilians remained unclear. The experience of Kosovo showed that without threat of a ground invasion, a regime can disperse and disguise its forces. Lacking unity, training, and equipment, the Libyan opposition hardly seemed capable of standing up to Qaddafi's troops even if the regime could no longer attack rebels from the air. Policymakers feared mission creep leading to a ground war, a backlash against the United States in the Arab world, and the possibility of Islamists controlling post-war Libya. All of these factors led journalist Matt Gurney to proclaim in a February 24 editorial titled (ironically as it turned out), "Why America won't bomb Libya" that "the imposition of a no-fly zone is unlikely to happen unless the situation in Libya worsens dramatically. Taking on the mission entails too much downside for the nations that would have to be involved."[87] The situation did worsen, but so had the situations in Bahrain, Yemen, and Syria, where the United States did not get involved.

Why, then, did the Obama administration decide to intervene in the Libyan civil war? In an address to the nation from the National Defense University on March 28, 2011, the President cited humanitarian reasons for intervening, foremost among them desire to prevent a massacre of civilians in Benghazi.[88] Despite concern for the well-being of Libyan civilians, the Obama administration remained reluctant to intervene militarily in Libya and did so only at the request of the Arab League, with UN approval and at the urging of France and Britain.[89] A desire to support NATO allies, which had supported the United States over the years, may thus have influenced the President's thinking.

Of the two countries sounding the drum beat for intervention France had the greatest strategic interest in Libya. "Europe is in the frontline" facing the upheaval in North Africa, French President Nicolas Sarkozy stated. He added that the continent could not ignore "important migratory movements," an oblique reference to Libyan refugees fleeing to Europe.[90] Sarkozy may also have been motivated by his desire to see France play a leading role in international affairs and a wish to give his sagging approval ratings at home a boost.[91] Britain had no immediate strategic interest in Libya, and Prime Minister David Cameron needed no increase in his popularity. Like his French counterpart, however, Cameron may simply have wished to be on the right side of history as a sea change swept the Arab world.[92] The British also had no love for Qaddafi, who had trained and supplied members of the Irish Republican Army during the troubles in Northern Ireland.

By mid-March 2011, all the conditions set by President Obama for intervention had been met. The Arab League had requested action, the UN Security Council had passed the requisite resolution approving it, and

Britain and France agreed to take the lead, although everyone knew that the United States would contribute the largest percentage of assets needed for the mission. The President made clear from the outset that he would not deploy ground troops to Libya, which the UN resolution clearly forbade. He did, however, allow CIA operatives to enter Libya to gather targeting intelligence for the air campaign. The British and French supplied and probably trained the revolutionaries and may also have had covert assets on the ground.

Even though the chances of suffering casualties in an air campaign would be small, the mission did carry significant political risk. As the Kosovo War had made abundantly clear, air campaigns may take a long time to achieve results, especially if the enemy realizes that the nation or coalition launching it will not send in ground forces. The longer the air campaign takes, the more civilians, the very people, the intervention allegedly seeks to protect, will suffer. In such a situation, the Obama administration could face the difficult choice of being drawn into a ground war or accepting failure. Fortunately, the Libyan rebels were more numerous and better equipped than the KLA, since many of them had defected from the Libyan armed forces. They also controlled the eastern port city of Benghazi through which they could receive supplies. It thus took less time to mold them into an effective force capable of overthrowing Qaddafi than it might otherwise have done. The United States thus had no need to participate in a follow-on mission, so the exit strategy consisted of the end of air action once its objective had been achieved.

The Libyan mission commenced amid more uncertainty than the operations in Haiti, Bosnia, or Kosovo. In terms of military assets and personnel, the United

States risked little. There was, however, no guarantee that an air campaign would enable the rebels to defeat the Qaddafi regime. The intervention carried significant political risk, especially during an election year. Defeat of the rebels would have left the President open to a charge of weakness, which Republican challenger Mitt Romney leveled anyway. Success carried with it the greater risk that the new Libyan regime would be anti-Western. The high political risk-to-gain ratio suggests that Washington can mount a successful intervention even without a compelling political reason to do so, *provided* that mission does not endanger Americans and does not last long.

NONINTERVENTIONS

A study of armed intervention requires consideration of civil conflicts in which the United States might have intervened but chose not to do so. Four such opportunities have occurred during the post-Cold War era: Rwanda (1994), Bahrain (2011), Yemen (2011), and Syria (2011-12). The Rwandan genocide occurred 1 year after Somalia, and the other three conflicts began at almost the same time as the Libyan mission. They were part of the larger upheaval known as the Arab Spring. Each of these conflicts stood juxtaposed to a major American intervention, raising moral and political questions as to why the United States chose to get involved in one crisis but not another.

The cases of Bahrain and Yemen are fairly straight forward. In Bahrain, the government did crackdown on dissidents, but for a very short period of time and with minimal loss of life. Reprehensible though human rights violations by its government were, the country never degenerated into civil war. The emirate could also plausibly claim that Iran had instigated the protests, which remained confined to its Shi'a population. Conditions in Bahrain never reached anything like the level of violence in Somalia, Bosnia, Kosovo, or Libya. Yemen is a fragile state with deep tribal divisions and a strong al-Qaeda presence in rural areas. Intervening there would have presented the United States with a problem as intractable as Afghanistan. In any event, the opposition did succeed in forcing out the president without the need of American intervention. Rwanda and Syria, on the other hand, were far more complex cases requiring fuller discussion. The same analytical questions used by this analysis to examine American interventions can shed light on why the United States did not intervene in these two countries.

Rwanda.

The Rwandan genocide of 1994 is one of the great tragedies of the late 20th century. A ceasefire following 3 years of civil war between the forces of the majority Hutu government and rebels from the ethnic Tutsi minority collapsed following the death of the Hutu president when his plane was shot down on April 6, presumably by Tutsi rebels. Hutu extremists backed by the army unleashed a wave of killings that took the lives of perhaps half a million Tutsis and some 157,000 Hutus.[93] The small UN Assistance Mission for Rwanda (UNAMIR) deployed under a Chapter 6 peacekeeping mandate lacked the numbers, the equipment, and the authority to stop the killing. UNAMIR's request for more troops and the freedom to use them fell on deaf ears in New York and the Western capitals.

The Western powers in general, and the United States in particular, have faced harsh criticism for their failure to intervene in the conflict. Canadian General Romeo Dallaire, commander of UNAMIR, has led a chorus of voices condemning western leaders for failing to stop the genocide. "Why is it that black Africans, sitting there getting slaughtered by the thousands, get nothing," he asked in a PBS interview. "Why is it when a bunch of white Europeans get slaughtered in Yugoslavia, you can't put enough capability in there?"[94] Dallaire has insisted ever since the tragedy unfolded that given 5,000 troops, he could have stopped the genocide. His assessment distorts American motives, grossly oversimplifies the situation as it unfolded in Rwanda during April and May of 1994, and is not entirely consistent with his own perceptions of events at the time.

The charge of indifference to African suffering based on racism does not hold up under close scrutiny. The United States had just led a massive intervention in Somalia motivated by nothing more than humanitarian concern. It also spent $43 million on humanitarian aid to Rwanda refugees after the conflict ended.[95] As for the UN, its largest mission prior to Bosnia was the 1960 intervention in the Congo. Contrary to Dallaire's assertion, the Clinton administration had not been eager to get involved in Yugoslavia, where it intervened only in the last few months of the conflict, long after most victims of that genocide were dead. Even then, American motives were not purely humanitarian, but also strategic. The United States was not averse to helping Africans, but it was leery of committing ground forces to intervene in a civil war. Airpower would have been useless in the face of mass killing by small groups dispersed throughout rural areas. The claim that the genocide could have been prevented with a prompt deployment of 5000 troops has also been challenged.[96] This conclusion rests on three questionable assumptions: that the United States knew genocide was unfolding in time to stop it, that 5,000 Soldiers would have been sufficient to stop the killing, and that these troops could have been deployed soon enough to have had a decisive effect.

Alan Kuperman argues quite persuasively that President Clinton could not have known that the killing in Rwanda amounted to genocide until April 20 at the earliest, by which time perhaps 250,000 people were already dead.[97] UN documents and media accounts support Kuperman's conclusion. In his April 20 report to the Security Council on the activities of UNAMIR, Secretary-General Boutros Boutros-Ghali noted that the death of the Rwandan president had provoked widespread killing "mainly in Kigali" and concluded that: "No reliable estimate of deaths has so far been available, but they could possibly number tens of thousands."[98] The report grossly underestimated the death toll and focused on the capital, where only 4 percent of Rwandans lived. On May 13, Boutros-Ghali submitted another report to the Security Council, describing the situation in Rwanda as a "civil conflict" and focusing on the refugee crisis it created, not on mass killing.[99] *Newsweek* also described the conflict as a civil war, albeit one in which armed gangs murdered civilians, but not one of systematic genocide by one group against another.[100] The article quotes Dallaire: "If we spend another three weeks cooped up here watching them pound each other, we'll have to reassess [whether to stay]."[101] Dallaire's choice of words suggests that he, too, viewed the struggle as a civil war and even seems to have considered withdrawal of the mission.

Whatever they thought in April, by mid-May neither the UN nor western leaders could deny that Hutus were murdering Tutsi men, women, and children on a large scale. Once world leaders realized that genocide was occurring, the next two questions raised by critics of nonintervention become pertinent: would 5,000 troops have stopped the killing, and could they have been deployed in time to do so? Kuperman argues persuasively that 5,000 adequately equipped solders with the necessary logistic support could not have deployed in less than a few weeks, and that while this deployment might have stabilized Kigali, it could not have stopped most of the killing in the countryside, where more than 90 percent of Rwandans lived.[102] Even he admits, however, that timely intervention could have saved perhaps 125,000 people.[103]

Considering whether American intervention could have saved 125,000 victims or stopped the genocide entirely, still leaves unanswered the question of why the Clinton administration chose not to get involved in Rwanda, while intervening in Haiti the same year and Bosnia the following. The disaster of Somali offers part of the explanation. Since Vietnam, the United States had avoided intervening with ground forces in civil conflicts with the exception of El Salvador, where it deployed only a small number of advisors. In the context of the post-Vietnam era, Somalia, not Rwanda, is the outlier. Embarrassment over failure to intervene in Rwanda may also explain the increased willingness to go to Bosnia and Kosovo, as the African tragedy spurred a new American consciousness of the need to prevent and/or halt genocide.[104]

The analytical framework of this analysis provides a compelling argument as to why the United States did not intervene in Rwanda. No compelling U.S. interests were at stake. The Clinton administration did not have the means to stop the genocide, which was well underway before Washington even knew it was occurring. Deploying troops to the capital would certainly have saved some lives, but most of the killing took place in the countryside. To occupy all the affected areas would have required far more troops than Dallaire believed and would have embroiled the United States in a situation much like Somalia without a clear exit strategy.

Syria.

The Syrian civil war began as a series of protests in Deraa in March 2011, sparked by the upheaval in Tunisia the previous month. When protesters demanding democratic reform faced repression by the Syrian army, unrest spread to other cities and initiated an increasing cycle of violence. Members of the armed forces and the civilian government defected to the opposition, whose demands had escalated to removing President Bashar al-Assad from power. The disparate elements of the opposition formed the Syrian National Council and insurgent military forces coalesced into the Free Syrian Army (FSA). The FSA is not a coherent fighting force but an umbrella organization of militias and paramilitary organizations of very uneven quality.[105] Conservative estimates number the FSA at 7,000 fighters, whose weapons come from Syrian military defectors and black-market arms sales via Iraq, Lebanon, and Turkey.[106]

Fighting has taken the form of ambushes, street battles, and guerrilla warfare, with the FSA liberating neighborhoods and even entire towns. Assad has responded with indiscriminate shelling, air attacks and brutal reprisals against entire communities. The civil war also has an ethnic dimension, as FSA fighters belong to the Sunni majority, and government forces, particularly the ruthless paramilitary groups, come from Assad's Allawi Shi'a Sect. By late July 2012, the death toll had exceeded 19,000, most of them civilians killed by government forces.[107] On August 15, 2012, the UN High Commissioner for Refugees reported the number of refugees fleeing the conflict at 155,753.[108] Since this number does not include internally displaced persons or unregistered refugees, the number of people driven from their homes by the fighting is probably much higher.

The Syrian Civil War has many of the characteristics and conditions that drew the United States and its allies into Libya. Nonetheless, the Obama administration has confined its efforts to demanding Assad relinquish power and calling for UN sanctions, which Russia and China consistently block. Lack of a UN resolution approving intervention is most often stated as the reason for inaction. Since the absence of such approval did not stop President Clinton from intervening in Kosovo, however, American reluctance must be in part ascribed to other factors. Because the conflict in Syria is still unfolding, however, assessing the motives of the Obama administration for not intervening in it requires speculation.

Some conclusions can, nonetheless, be drawn with confidence. Embarking on a risky foreign policy venture during a presidential election is almost always a bad idea. George H. W. Bush only intervened in Somalia after he had lost the 1992 election. Obama's willingness to tackle health care reform and authorize a raid on Osama bin Laden's hideout deep in Pakistan demonstrates his willingness to take risks. Absent other inhibiting factors, he might have chanced intervening in Syria by using airpower as he had done in Libya, but he was not about to do so during a close re-election campaign. His re-election has lessened partisan concerns, but has not removed the other impediments to intervention.

Unlike the Libyan civil war, the Syrian conflict presents a complex problem in a volatile region of the world. Missteps in the Middle East can have far more serious consequences than could those in North Africa or the Balkans. Saudi Arabia and the Gulf States back the rebels, as does Turkey. Iran sides with Syria, which also enjoys support from Russia. Israel has no love for the Damascus regime but wonders whether the devil it knows might not be better than the one it does not. The Assad family has, after all, kept Syria's border with Israel quiet for decades, even if they have also supported Hezbollah. The prospect of an Islamist regime ruling Syria combined with the new, less friendly one in Egypt makes Israel nervous. Uncertainty over the nature and stability of post-Assad Syria also bothers Washington, especially since opposition leaders have failed to guarantee that Islamists would not be part of any new government.[109] Anxiety increased in August 2012 when reports of al-Qaeda and other extremist groups aiding Syrian rebels surfaced.[110] These reports confirmed fears Secretary of State Hillary Clinton had expressed earlier in the year. "We have a very dangerous set of actors in the region," she told BBC news in February, "Al-Qaeda, Hamas, and those who are on our terrorist list, to be sure, supporting—claiming to support the opposition."[111] Fear that weapons supplied to the FSA might fall into the hands of terrorists has made the administration wary of arming them. Washington also fears that supplying weapons to the opposition might induce Russia and/or Iran to counter with more aid to the regime, thus escalating the civil war and increasing the suffering and loss of life.[112]

For all these reasons, the United States has eschewed direct involvement in the Syrian civil war and, barring some unforeseen change in circumstances, will probably continue to do so. In the unlikely event that Vladimir Putin withdraws his support for Assad, the United States might be able to get UN approval for a no-fly zone to protect Syrian civilians, although it is unlikely that the Russians or the Chinese would allow such a mission to escalate into providing air cover for the rebels as happened in Libya. Should Iran become directly involved by sending military personnel into Syria to support the regime, the United States might perceive an existential threat to Israel and intervene unilaterally. Despite declaring that the use of chemical weapons represented a red line that Damascus dare not cross, Obama did not act on reports in April 2013 that Assad had made limited use of sarin gas. In all probability, the conflict will be resolved by the Syrians themselves with no probable outcome particularly favorable to Western interests. Any regime that replaces Assad will no doubt bitterly resent America's failure to support the revolution. If Assad wins, his weakened regime will depend even more on Iran. Neither of these scenarios bodes well for regional stability.

PATTERNS AND POSSIBILITIES

The cases examined herein reveal broad patterns from which specific recommendations about the nature and conduct of interventions might be derived. Properly applied, these lessons might offer some guidance on when and how to conduct interventions. Past campaigns cannot, however, provide a blueprint for future ones. History offers lessons, but it does not, contrary to the popular cliché, repeat itself. Those lessons must be learned and creatively applied to each new situation.

Where to Intervene.

Democratic and Republican Presidents have insisted that American values as well as political interests shape U.S. foreign policy. This claim has been a cornerstone of political discourse for much of the Republic's history. The United States has developed its own unique version of just war theory, claiming since the early 19th century that wars, even wars of conquest, must "liberate the oppressed and expand the sphere of freedom."[113] The cases examined here, however, suggest that values alone rarely provide sufficient incentive for intervention. Only in the case of Somalia can it be argued that humanitarian motives alone persuaded the White House to intervene. As a lame-duck President, George H. W. Bush had the luxury of acting purely on principle. Not only did that operation end very badly, but its failure cast a very long shadow. The Somalia debacle probably affected the decision to stay out of Rwanda, where humanitarianism alone would have compelled intervention, and may have delayed intervention in Bosnia. Presidents may, however, mount limited humanitarian interventions using military force provided they manage the risk to service personnel and keep the intervention short and focused. UNITAF fit this pattern in Somalia, even if the American commitment to UNOSOM II did not. Humanitarian considerations figured prominently in the Libyan mission, but the Obama administration confined the intervention to a low-risk, air campaign.

In most cases intervention has to be justified based upon pragmatic as well as altruistic grounds. In every case but Somalia, a compelling U.S. interest underlay the decision to get involved even when desire to alleviate suffering became a consideration. In the cases of Bosnia and Kosovo, the need to promote regional stability and buttress the credibility of NATO combined with a commitment to preventing genocide. Absent such strategic considerations, stopping genocide did not provide sufficient grounds for intervening in Rwanda. The Obama administration certainly wished to prevent Muammar Qaddafi slaughtering his own people, but it also acted as much out of a commitment to its NATO allies as from a desire to prevent the deaths of innocent Libyans.

Even when humanitarian sentiment and strategic interests combine, they do not always provide sufficient grounds for intervention, as the case of Syria makes painfully clear. Washington has watched with growing concern as the country slides deeper into civil war and President Bashir Assad uses increasingly indiscriminate force against his own people. The White House has also worried about the destabilizing effect of Syria imploding in one of the most volatile areas of the world. The President seems to support enforcement of a no-fly zone over the country and might even allow direct air action against Syrian regime forces. Strategic and humanitarian considerations have thus favored intervention. International and domestic considerations, however, have not. Feeling misled in Libya by the NATO allies, Russia and China have made it clear that they will not support intervention in Syria. Russia in particular poses as Assad's protector, which emboldens the dictator. Furthermore, as the situation in that country deteriorated, the United States entered a presidential election year. Facing a tough challenge from Republican Mitt Romney, President Obama was reluctant to risk an intervention that would be unpopular with both Congress and the American people. Now that he has been re-elected, his reluctance has not disappeared. War weariness from the long conflicts in Iraq and Afghanistan and concern over the economy has made the American public leery of another intervention that might be open-ended and costly in both lives and money.

While domestic politics may be a major consideration when contemplating intervention during an election year, it is rarely a decisive factor at other times. None of the interventions studied here was popular with the possible (and ironic) exception of Somalia. Even then, the initial desire to alleviate famine rapidly waned as the mission dragged on with no clear end in sight. The American people have never had much patience for foreign wars unless vital U.S. interests were clearly at stake. Lack of public or even congressional support has not stopped Presidents from intervening in foreign crises. To intervene effectively, however, they needed to prevent lack of support turning to outright opposition. Apathy is relatively easy to overcome; hostility is not. As the case of Somalia clearly indicates, opposition increases with the duration of the mission and the rise in casualties. While Congress complains about the financial cost of missions, the long deployments to Bosnia and Kosovo produced no public outcry to bring the troops home. To the American public, blood means more than treasure. IFOR/SFOR and KFOR lasted several years, but as they soon became little more than confidence-building/stability missions that suffered virtually no casualties and represented no serious drain on military manpower, they ruffled few feathers at home.

When to Intervene.

Deciding when to intervene can be as tricky as choosing where to get involved. The old saying that an ounce of prevention is worth a pound of cure holds true for foreign policy as for any other human endeavor, but the United States can seldom justify meddling in the affairs of a sovereign state before a crisis requires doing so. Somalia and Bosnia were failed states before the United States intervened. Haiti had descended into chaos, and Kosovo faced an impending genocide. The United States did not initially support Kosovar independence. Only in the case of Libya, did Washington reluctantly agree to back a revolutionary movement that overthrew the existing government.

As a crisis unfolds, there may be an optimal time to intervene. Unfortunately, optimal for the intervening power may not be the same as optimal for the people in the war-torn country. Bosnia provides an example of this dilemma. Had the United States intervened earlier, it would have saved many lives. By waiting until Bosnian Serb power had reached its peak and begun to decline, however, the Clinton administration intervened under circumstances that assured success in a short kinetic operation with little risk of casualties. The Croat and Bosniac ground offensives had created a tipping point that allowed a brief air campaign to achieve decisive results.

In most cases, the United States had to allow diplomatic efforts to play out before it intervened militarily. A lengthy but ultimately futile peace process preceded the interventions in Haiti, Bosnia, and Kosovo.

Bashir Assad has allowed fact-finding and observer missions to forestall intervention as did Slobodan Milošević. Muammar Qaddafi never got the chance to dither, but the NATO allies offered him the opportunity to leave the country before being defeated and summarily executed. The United States seldom controls precisely when it can intervene, and recognizing the best time to do so is always clearer in hindsight. However, the cases examined here suggests two optimal periods, depending on circumstances. In cases of humanitarian crisis (famine, natural disasters, etc.), early intervention offers better chances of success than belated involvement. Early intervention is also desirable when the goal is to defend a threatened regime or support a rebellion. In cases of civil war in which the goal is to force both sides into a negotiated settlement, it may be desirable to wait until the belligerents have reached a stalemate. The odds that an American President will be able to determine precisely the best time to intervene in the fluid situation of a crisis are, however, remote. Understanding the dynamics of conflicts and crises may help policymakers time interventions more effectively.

How to Intervene.

The manner in which the United States conducts an intervention will affect its course and outcome. Intervening as part of an alliance or coalition has advantages and disadvantages. Alliances and coalitions usually limit the nature of intervention, producing least-common-denominator strategy. On the other hand, they multiply resources and can convey greater legitimacy on the intervention. The UN has the greatest ability to confer legitimacy on military operations, although getting its approval for intervention has become more difficult. The missions to Haiti, Bosnia, and Somalia operated under UN mandates. Technically the Libyan operation did as well, although Russia and China have argued with some justification that the NATO allies distorted the true intent of that mandate. The Kosovo mission lacked UN approval but enjoyed widespread international support, at least in the West. In Haiti, the United States had the best of both worlds: UN approval for a multilateral mission that was for all intents and purposes unilateral.[114]

The refusal of the United States and its NATO allies to intervene in Syria without UN approval suggests that international support is more than window dressing. Unless it faces an immediate threat or sees a significant strategic interest challenged, the United States will probably not intervene anywhere unilaterally with the possible exception of its historic sphere of influence in the Caribbean and Central America. Even then, as the intervention in Haiti suggests, Washington will try to seek international support for intervention even in this region long considered America's backyard.

The cases examined suggest that the intervention in Haiti occurred under the most favorable circumstances. The United States enjoyed international support for what it billed as a multilateral mission without any of the constraints that normally go with coalition operations. The mission became truly multilateral only after the permissive entry of U.S. forces had accomplished the goal of removing the Haitian dictator and restoring order to the island. As desirable as the circumstances of this intervention were, they will probably not be duplicated in future crises or conflicts.

Whether acting unilaterally or as part of a coalition, the United States must chose the precise means for intervening in each case. From a purely military point of view, it makes sense to use a maximum amount of force. The mere threat of a U.S. invasion compelled General Cédras to relinquish power in Haiti without a shot being fired. By contrast, President Clinton's announcement that he would not invade Kosovo with ground troops emboldened Milošević into believing he could survive an air campaign, which he might have done were it not for the fact that preserving NATO credibility became a major mission objective. Since interventions are classified as "operations other than war" in U.S. military doctrine, however, they will be mounted using limited U.S. assets. Somalia involved air, land, and naval forces; Haiti was a permissive entry; Bosnia and Kosovo were air campaigns followed by the permissive deployment of stability missions; and Libya was an air campaign with no follow-on ground deployment. What assets the United States can use will depend on the circumstances, but committing too few military personnel, especially when ground troops might be directly engaged in hostilities, is always a bad idea. Leaving aside the wisdom of trying to capture Aidid in Somalia, the U.S. contingent lacked the armor necessary to support its Special Forces, and this weakness had disastrous consequences.

The cases examined suggest that air power is, politically at least, the most effective means of intervention, counterintuitive though that conclusion may be. Despite improved guidance systems, manned aircraft and cruise missiles are still relatively blunt instruments, and even drones have trouble distinguishing friend from foe in urban areas. An enemy who realizes he will only be attacked from the air can disperse his assets and disguise his soldiers. Air campaigns (short of wholesale bombing, which the United States usually will not do) without ground troops take much longer to produce results. In the case of Bosnia, air action achieved decisive results rapidly because Bosniac troops, and the NATO rapid reaction force could exploit it. In Kosovo, an air campaign that was supposed to last at most a few weeks took 78 days to achieve results, during which time Kosovar civilians suffered terribly at the hands of Serbian forces. A revived KLA and the threat of a NATO invasion contributed to success. The air campaign against Libya also took months to achieve results, even with revolutionary forces on the ground.

Despite these drawbacks, however, airpower has two definite political advantages: it puts few Americans at risk; and it seldom creates the legacy of bitterness produced by ground troops. The cases examined suggest that occupation, not the level of force used to intervene, produces the anti-American feelings that can rapidly turn violent. Ordinary Somalis may have appreciated the famine relief effort of 1992-93, but the warring factions did not welcome into their country either U.S. or UN troops, which they considered just one more armed group in a multifaceted civil conflict. The longer the troops remained, the more resentment at their presence increased. Far less anti-American feeling has arisen in Libya, where no ground troops deployed. The attack on the U.S. consulate in Benghazi was probably the work of a terrorist group, not a reflection of anti-American feeling throughout the country. Americans are appreciated in Bosnia and positively loved in Kosovo, but in those places, U.S. troops entered permissively as part of a stabilization force following an air campaign. Politically at least, the ideal scenario for U.S. intervention (besides completely permissive entry as in Haiti) is American airpower deployed in support of ground forces provided by coalition or alliance partners, which occurred in both Bosnia and Libya.

Unfortunately, what is best for the United States is not always best for the people on whose behalf the intervention is mounted. Air campaigns to protect civilians or to support rebellion must be selective, but even when they are conducted with great restraint, they still cause civilian casualties. They also take time to achieve results, and during that time, the regime continues to kill innocent people. Problematic though it is, however, under some circumstances air action may be the only way the White House can mount an intervention acceptable to Congress and the American people.

Follow-on Missions.

Interventions rarely conclude with the end of hostilities. The instability and political strife that prompted the intervention usually necessitate a protracted follow-on mission. U.S. doctrine conceptualizes intervention using a five-phase model, ranging from deterrence (Phase 1) through military operations (Phases 2 and 3) to stabilization and restoration of normal government (Phases 4 and 5).[115] The United States in general and the U.S. military in particular have a strong dislike for Phase 4 Stability Operations. Dubbed by its critics and proponents alike as "nation building," Phase 4 involves a multiplicity of tasks. Although few of these tasks are military in nature, performing them often requires the kind of security only soldiers can provide. The human terrain in which stability operations take place precludes using most of the assets of a high-tech, maneuver-warfare army. Troops may come under fire from insurgents or malcontents they cannot easily identify because they hide within a sullen or even hostile civilian population. Under such circumstances, soldiers can quickly go from being welcomed as liberators to being resented as occupiers, which occurred in both Iraq and Afghanistan. Phase 4 operations also create a "you-broke-it, you-bought it" situation that makes it hard for American forces to withdraw in a timely manner.

The United States, thus, understandably avoids direct involvement in Phase 4 stability operations and tries to limit its role when such avoidance proves impossible. Somalia provides a lesson of what can happen when Washington commits American troops to an open-ended stability operation. The Clinton administration did not repeat the mistake it made in East Africa. When American forces in Haiti found themselves having to assume a law and order role for which they were not prepared, they quickly adjusted their rules of engagement and promptly handed over the UN mission responsibility for Phase 4, contributing only a small number of personnel to that operation. The United States did commit a large troop contingent to both IFOR and KFOR but only after an air campaign compelled permissive entry of those missions into Bosnia and Kosovo respectively. Once it deployed American troops, however, the White House kept the U.S. contingents on a very short leash. Robust rules of engagement, rigorous force protection measures, and a narrow definition of the mission prevented casualties. In the case of Libya, of course, the United States deployed no troops at all.

Exit Strategy.

Disengaging from interventions can be extraordi-
narily difficult. Fragile states easily degenerate into
failed ones, and the nation, alliance, or coalition that
successfully intervenes often finds itself saddled with
an expensive nation-building mission that can last
years. Given the American dislike for both nation-
building and open-ended commitments, a viable exit
strategy (preferably right after kinetic operations
cease) should be part of any intervention plan. In all
but one of the interventions examined here, the United States had either an exit strategy or a plan for keep-
ing American ground troops out of harm's way, while
reducing their numbers as soon as possible.

As previously noted, the intervention in Somalia
might for the sake of academic argument be viewed
as two operations. UNITAF did have a clear exit strategy. The Marines planned to remain long enough to
secure delivery of humanitarian aid and then withdraw. They accomplished their goal in a short, decisive operation from December 1992 to May 1994. Had
the United States withdrawn all of its force at the end
of that period, the mission would have been heralded
as a success. Instead, the Clinton administration chose
to keep some American forces in country as part of a
rather open-ended UN peace operation. The new mission had the broad goal of restoring normal political
life but no clear plan for achieving it. Somalis soon
perceived UNOSOM II as yet another armed faction,
and the October 3 "Blackhawk Down" incident soon
followed. The United States did pull its troops out
soon after the debacle, but it did so in a manner that
looked more like an ignominious withdrawal than a
decisive exit strategy.

BALANCING CONSIDERATIONS

The questions posed by this analysis all factor into considering whether or not to mount an armed intervention. They are not always, however, of equal importance, and they may interact in different ways under different circumstances. Maintaining political will by sustaining public support for operations would appear to be the most critical issue in mounting an intervention, but the cases examined herein do not support such a simple conclusion. To begin with, political will does not always require popular support. None of the interventions examined here was particularly popular. The Pew Research Center determined that in March 2011, only 27 percent of Americans felt the United States had an obligation to "do something about" the fighting in Libya.[116] In March 1999, 47 percent felt Washington should get involved in Kosovo, but only 30 percent felt that way about Bosnia in June 1995.[117] With less than a third of the American public behind him, President Clinton intervened successfully in Kosovo and President Obama in Libya. Although more than half of Americans (51 percent) favored taking action to stop the killing in Darfur in December 2006, President Bush did not even consider such action.[118]

Presidents may not need to have popular support for intervention, but they need to avoid opposition. Opposition arises most quickly when American servicemen and women die. The Somalia mission provides the best illustration. Support for the intervention went from a high of 84 percent in January 1993 to a low of 33 percent after the October 3 "Blackhawk Down" incident.[119] The decline in support, however, may not have reflected a simple correlation with rising casualties, but revealed instead unhappiness over deaths in a mission whose goals Americans no longer supported.[120] In other words, the public accepted casualties incurred while saving Somalia children from starvation, but did not approve loss of life suffered trying to capture Aidid. Matthew Baum has postulated a further explanation for the role of public opinion in military interventions. He suggests that public opinion will have the greatest impact on presidential behavior during an intervention in which media attention is intense, the stakes for the United States are low, and the President lacks confidence in the outcome of the mission—conditions that existed in the case of Somalia after the October 3 incident.[121] These findings and the cases examined suggest that public opinion matters, but that its precise impact on decisionmaking is complex and difficult to track. It seems to matter most when a mission goes badly.

The likelihood of casualties and therefore of adverse public opinion depends in part upon the means used to intervene. As the cases of Bosnia, Kosovo, and Libya illustrate, air action costs few, if any, American lives and, perhaps ironically, produces less of a backlash in the country being bombed than does occupation by ground forces. This advantage suggests that Presidents will opt for air action whenever possible. However, Phase 4 stability operations cannot be conducted with cruise missiles, attack aircraft, or predator drones. The cases examined suggest that U.S. participation in Phase 4, follow-on stability operations creates no serious problems for policymakers, strategists, or the American public provided they do not result in casualties.

IMPLICATIONS FOR U.S. LAND POWER

An analysis of this type would be incomplete without consideration of its implications for the future of U.S. landpower, particularly the size and composition of the army. With the Iraq war over and the conflict in Afghanistan winding down, a reduction in military spending and/or reallocation of defense resources seems likely. The nature of the U.S. military in the next decade will depend on the strategic tasks given it by the political leadership. The threat posed by China has already led to a shift in resources to the Pacific, a trend that seems likely to continue. Those resources will be primarily naval and air assets, but the required additional allocations for the Navy and Air Force could pull resources from the Army. Land forces will, of course, remain a vital component of the U.S. military, but their strategic role will be diverse and challenging, covering contingencies ranging from counterterrorism through insurgency to mid-level conventional war. In some cases these contingencies will be present in challenging combinations generically dubbed "hybrid wars."[122] The likelihood of each contingency for the foreseeable future will impact the size and composition of land forces.

The most recent *Quadrennial Defense Review* (QDR) insists that in addition to preparing for conventional war:

> U.S. ground forces will remain capable of full-spectrum operations, with continued focus on capabilities to conduct effective and sustained counterinsurgency, stability, and counterterrorist operations alone and in concert with partners.[123]

A Strategic Studies Institute (SSI) report published the previous year drew a similar conclusion: "Armed stabilization may be the next most common and most important major combat operation (MCO) for DoD [Department of Defense] land forces."[124] As the cases analyzed here suggest, some form of Phase 4 stability operations often follow armed intervention into the affairs of a foreign state. Such operations require substantial deployments of ground forces performing a multitude of tasks for a sustained period of time. To carry out such missions, American forces will:

> require capabilities to create a secure environment in fragile states in support of local authorities and, if necessary, to support civil authorities in providing essential government services, restoring emergency infrastructure, and supplying humanitarian relief.[125]

The QDR makes two specific recommendations designed to enhance the ability of the U.S. military to conduct unconventional operations: "Increase COIN [counterinsurgency], stability operations, and CT [counterterrorism] competency and capacity in general purpose forces;" and "Expand civil affairs capacity."[126] The SSI study recommends that land forces "optimize for the limited armed stabilization of crippled states."[127]

These and many other studies address the types of operations U.S. land forces will perform without addressing the size of the army. They also leave unaddressed the balance of conventional versus unconventional capability. Traditional wisdom has it that preparing Soldiers to conduct the one type of operation degrades their ability to conduct the other. At least one study challenges this wisdom, arguing that it is based on the fallacious assumption that U.S. forces are slower to transition than their foes and so must choose either a conventional or an unconventional focus.[128] The experience of Afghanistan and Iraq supports the conclusion of this study, since both wars demonstrated the ability of American troops to adapt to changing circumstances. These reports and the findings of this Paper point to the same important lesson: whatever the size of the U.S. Army, it must train two-speed Soldiers equally capable of both conventional and unconventional operations. There will, of course, always be the need for specialized units. President Obama's commitment to expanding Special Forces will enhance the U.S. military's ability to conduct a broad range of missions as will expansion of civil affairs units, which occurred during the Iraq and Afghan Wars and will probably continue.

CONCLUSION

Making recommendations to guide future policy is much harder than identifying patterns and deriving lessons from past campaigns. Much depends on the historical circumstances in which events unfold. In the aftermath of Vietnam, the U.S. military and the American public had little stomach for protracted intervention. The 1980s saw short, decisive actions in Grenada and Panama, the small covert operation in Nicaragua, and the advisory mission in El Salvador. During the decade following the collapse of the Berlin Wall, the United States mounted several large-scale interventions. With the war in Iraq over and the 2014 date for withdrawal of U.S. combat forces from Afghanistan fast approaching, the country appears to be entering another period of disillusionment with nation-building. War-weariness combined with the tremendous cost of the two lengthy conflicts and the weak state of the American economy will make it harder for the President to intervene in the internal affairs of other states unless major strategic interests are clearly and demonstratively at stake.

In the event the United States finds it necessary to intervene for either strategic or humanitarian reasons (or a combination of the two), however, this Paper suggests a reasonable approach to such missions. Whenever possible, the United States should intervene on behalf of a coalition, preferably with UN approval. It should confine its contribution to providing air power, high tech support, logistics, and perhaps covert operatives. This approach worked well in Bosnia, Kosovo, and Libya. The United States suffered no combat casualties in any of these conflicts, and in none of these countries have people exhibited the widespread anti-Americanism that followed the occupations of Somalia, Afghanistan, and Iraq. It must be clearly understood, however, that no air campaign can be purely defensive. No-fly zones can only be imposed through gaining air supremacy, which requires destroying the enemy's air defense system. Also, without an opposition movement on the ground or allies willing to deploy ground troops, air action alone will probably not achieve decisive results.

However much it may wish to avoid such a mission, there will be times when the United States finds it necessary or desirable to intervene in a civil conflict or humanitarian crisis with ground forces. In the case of an insurgency threatening a friendly government, intervention may best be done with Special Operations Forces. When a humanitarian crisis occurs in a weak or failed state, intervention may require deployment of a more substantial mission. In such a situation, the case of UNITAF in Somalia provides the best example of how to proceed. The intervening force should be large, heavily armed, and have clear, robust rules of engagement. The mission should have a definite, achievable goal, a reasonable time limit, and a sound exit strategy. While it may not always be possible to have such precise control of the variables in an operation, Washington should be able to anticipate and plan for such eventualities. Controlled evolution of a mission is different than uncontrolled mission creep. The Black Hawk Down incident would not have happened had the Clinton administration stuck to the original goal of alleviating famine and not gotten drawn into arresting a warlord. The mission would then have ended in the spring of 1993 and been deemed a success.

In cases where the intervention takes the form of a post-conflict stability operation, a much larger force can safely be deployed as occurred in both Bosnia and Kosovo. Even then, however, the U.S. contingent should be kept as small as possible, steadily reduced in size, and withdrawn as soon as it reasonably can be. The more American Soldiers on the ground, the greater the likelihood of something going wrong. The longer U.S. troops stay in a country, the sooner their presence will be resented.

Intervention for reasons other than clear, immediate self-interest will probably remain unpopular with the American public for the foreseeable future. This unpopularity will not, however, make such missions go away. Presidents have to consider the national interest in terms far more subtle and nuanced than those of the average voter. That interest will surely require the United States to intervene in a civil conflict or humanitarian emergency somewhere in the world during the next decade. The success of that intervention will depend on how well it is planned and executed in light of the questions raised herein.

ENDNOTES

1. The best account of this conflict is Brain McAllister Linn, *The US Army and the Philippine War, 1899-1902*, Chapel Hill, NC: University of North Carolina Press, 1989.

2. Merritt Edson published his account in three installments in "The Coco Patrol," *Marine Corps Gazette*, August 1936, November 1936, February 1937; *Small Wars Manual, United States Marine Corps*, Washington, DC: Government Printing Office (GPO), 1940; Reprint Ed., 1987.

3. Abraham F. Lowenthal, "The United States and the Dominican Republic to 1965: Background to Intervention," *Caribbean Studies*, Vol. 10, No. 2, July, 1970, pp. 33-34.

4. Walter H. Posner, "The Marines in Haiti, 1915-1922," *The Americas*, Vol. 20, No. 3, January 1964, pp. pp. 231-266.

5. Michael McClintock, *Instruments of Statecraft: U.S. Guerrilla Warfare, Counterinsurgency, and Terrorism, 1940-1990*, New York: Pantheon Books, 1992, p. 13.

6. Andrew J. Birtle, *U.S. Army Counterinsurgency and Contingency Operations Doctrine, 1942-1976*, Washington, DC: GPO, 2006, pp. 65-66.

7. Peter L. Hahn, "Securing the Middle East: the Eisenhower Doctrine of 1957," *Presidential Studies Quarterly*, Vol. 36, No. 1, Presidential Doctrines, March 2006, p. 44.

8. Lowenthal, "The United States and the Dominican Republic to 1965," p. 53.

9. Andrew Krepinevich, *The Army and the Vietnam War*, Baltimore, MD: Johns Hopkins Press, 1986, p. 197.

10. Peter Dunn, "The American Army: the Vietnam War, 1965-1973," Ian Beckett and John Pimlott, eds., *Armed Forces and Modern Counterinsurgency,* New York: St. Martin's Press, 1985, p. 77.

11. Richard M. Nixon, Speech on Vietnamization, November 3, 1969, available from *vietnam.vassar.edu/overview/doc14.html.*

12. See for example, *U.S. Army Field Manual 31-20-3, Foreign Internal Defense: Tactics, Techniques, and Procedures for Special Forces,* Washington, DC: GPO, September 1994.

13. Thomas R. Mockaitis, *Resolving Insurgencies,* Carlisle, PA: Strategic Studies Institute, U.S. Army War College, 2011, pp. 52-56.

14. Michael J. Butler, "U.S. Military Intervention in Crisis, 1945-1994: An Empirical Inquiry of Just War Theory," *Journal of Conflict Resolution,* Vol. 48, No. 5, October 2004, p. 32.

15. Boutros Boutros-Ghali, *Agenda for Peace,* UN Document A/47/277 - S/24111, June 17, 1992.

16. Paul Diehl, *International Peacekeeping,* Urbana, IL: University of Illinois Press, 1993; William Durch, ed., *The Evolution of UN Peacekeeping: Case Studies and Comparative Analysis,* New York: St. Martin's Press, 1993; Thomas R. Mockaitis, *Peacekeeping and Intrastate Conflict: the Sword or the Olive Branch?* Westport, CT: Praeger, 1999.

17. Bruce W. Jentleson and Rebecca Britton, "Still Pretty Prudent: Post Cold-War American Public Opinion on the Use of Military Force," *The Journal of Conflict Resolution,* Vol. 42, No. 4, August 1998, pp. 395-417.

18. Jun Koga, "Where Do Third Parties Intervene? Third Parties' Domestic Institutions and Military Interventions in Civil Conflicts," *International Studies Quarterly,* Vol. 55, 2011, pp. 1143–1166.

19. James Meernik, "United States Military Intervention and the Promotion of Democracy," *Journal of Peace Research,* Vol. 33, No. 4, November 1996, pp. 391-402.

20. Stephen E. Gent, "Going in When it Counts: Military Intervention and the Outcome of Civil Conflicts," *International Studies Quarterly*, Vol. 52, 2008, pp. 713–735.

21. Benjamin O. Fordham, "The Influence of Military Capabilities on American Decisions to Use Force," *Journal of Conflict Resolution*, Vol. 48, No. 5, October 2004, pp. 632-656.

22. Jeffrey Pickering and Emizet F. Kisangani, "Political, Economic, and Social Consequences of Foreign Military Intervention," *Political Research Quarterly*, Vol. 59, No. 3, September 2006, pp. 363-376.

23. Doro Bush Koch, *My Father, My President: A Personal Account of the Life of George H. W. Bush,* New York: Wagner Books, 2006, pp. 426.

24. Bill Clinton, *My Life,* New York: Alfred A. Knopf, 2004, pp. 550; James A. Baker, III with Steve Fiffer, *"Work Hard, Study . . . and Keep out of Politics!"* New York: G. P. Putnam's Sons, 2006, pp. 307.

25. Abdulla Omar Mansur, "Contrary to a Nation: The Cancer of the Somali State," in Ali Jamal Ahmed, ed., *The Invention of Somalia,* Lawrenceville, NJ: The Red Sea Press, 1995, p. 107.

26. *Ibid.*

27. Samuel M. Makinda, *Seeking Peace from Chaos: Humanitarian Intervention in Somalia*, International Peace Academy Occasional Paper, Boulder, CO: Lynne Reiner, 1993, pp. 67-68.

28. Report on Activities of UNITAF, UN Document S/24976, December 17, 1993, p. 36.

29. Kenneth Allard, *Somalia Operations: Lessons Learned*, Washington, DC: NDU Press, 1995, p. 24.

30. Security Council Resolution 814, S/RES/814, 1993.

31. Report of the Secretary General on the Implementation of Security Council Resolution 837, S/RES/837, June 6, 1993, p. 3.

32. Patrick Sloyan, "Full of Tears and Grief; for Elite Commandos, Operation Ends in Disaster," *Newsday*, December 7, 1993, p. 1.

33. Further Report of the Secretary-General in Pursuance of Paragraph 18 of Resolution 814, 1993, UN Document S/26317, August 17, 1993.

34. *The World Fact Book*, Washington, DC: 2011, pp. available from *https://www.cia.gov/library/publications/the-world-factbook/geos/ha.html*.

35. Michael Bailey, Robert McGuire, and J. O'Neil G. Pouliot, "Haiti: Military-Police Partnership for Public Security," in Robert B. Oakley, Michael J. Dziedzic, and Eliot M. Goldberg, eds., Washington, DC: NDU Press, 1998, p. 215.

36. Sarah Meharg and Aleisha Arnusch, "Haiti: Military-Police Partnership for Public Security," *Security Sector Reform: A Case Study Approach to Transition and Capacity Building*, Carlisle, PA: Strategic Studies Institute, U.S. Army War College, 2010, p. 76.

37. Clinton, *My Life*, p. 616.

38. UN Security Council Resolution 940, S/RES/940, 31 July 1994, p. 2.

39. Meharag *et al.*, "Haiti," p. 219.

40. Sarah E. Kreps, "The 1994 Haiti Intervention: A Unilateral Operation in Multilateral Clothes," *The Journal of Strategic Studies*, Vol. 30, No. 3, June 2007, pp. 467.

41. *Ibid.*, pp. 449-474.

42. UN Security Council Resolution, S/RES/975, 1995, 30 January 1995.

43. Matjaž Klemencic, "The International Community's Response to the Yugoslav Crisis: 1989-1995," Presentation to Institute for Ethnic Studies in Ljubljana, Slovenia,

January 11, 2006, p. 1, unpublished manuscript available from *www.wilsoncenter.org/sites/default/files/MR320Klemencic.doc.*

44. UN Security Council Resolution, S/RES/713, 1991, 25 September 1991.

45. UN Security Council Resolution, S/RES/743, 1992, 21 February 1992.

46. Because the bodies were dumped in mass graves not exhumed until after the events, identifying the dead has been problematic, hence the wide range in casualty figures. As a result of its meticulous work, the International Committee of the Red Cross determined the minimum number of dead at 7,475. Helge Brunborg and Henrik Urdal, "Report on the Number of Missing and Dead from Srebrenica," File name: SUMMARY7.DOC, 12 February 2000.

47. Interoffice Memorandum, UN Peace Forces, HQ Zagreb to Special Representative of the Secretary-General, July 17, 1995, Lester Pearson Canadian Peacekeeping Center Archive.

48. Richard Holbrooke, *To End War,* New York: Harper Collins, 1998, p. 72.

49. James Gow, *Triumph of the Lack of Will,* New York: Columbia University Press, 1997, p. 275.

50. Outgoing Cable from Kofi Annan to Yasushi Akashi, Special Representative of the Secretary General (SRSG) for Bosnia-Herzegovina, July 19, 1995.

51. *Bosnia-Herzegovina. The U.S. Army's Role in Peace Operations 1995-2004,* Fort Leavenworth, KA: Center for Military History, 1997, p. 12, available from *www.history.army.mil/brochures/Bosnia-Herzegovina/Bosnia-Herzegovina.htm#Endeavor.*

52. "Operation Deliberate Force," available from *www.globalsecurity.org/military/ops/deliberate_force.htm.*

53. *Bosnia-Herzegovina,* p. 19.

54. *General Framework Agreement*, "Annex 1A: Agreement on the Military Aspects of the Peace Settlement," Article VI, available from *www.nato.int/ifor/gfa/gfa-an1a.htm*.

55. Clinton, *My Life*, p. 685.

56. *Ibid.*, p. 685.

57. "Still No Exit Strategy on Bosnia," *New York Times* online, September 25, 1997, available from *www.nytimes.com/1997/09/25/opinion/still-no-exit-strategy-on-bosnia.html*.

58. Clinton, *My Life*, p. 685.

59. Demographic figures are derived from 1991 census. *Kosovo Atlas*, Pristina, Kosovo: Office of the United Nations High Commissioner for Refugees (UNHCR), *et al.*, 2000, p. vi.

60. Howard Clark, *Civil Resistance in Kosovo*, London, UK: Pluto Press, 2000, pp. 95-121.

61. Miron Rezun, *Europe's Nightmare: The Struggle for Kosovo*, Westport, CT: Praeger, 2001, pp. 40, 45-46.

62. Casualty figures from Ivo Daalder and Michael O'Hanlon, *Winning Ugly: NATO's War to Save Kosovo*, Washington, DC: Brookings Institution Press, 2000, p. 27; refugee number from Miron Rezun, *Europe's Nightmare: The Struggle for Kosovo*, Westport, CT: Praeger, 2001, pp. 45-46.

63. Troop strength, *Kosovo/Kosova: As Seen, as Told*, Vol. II, Vienna, Austria: Office of Security and Cooperation in Europe, December 1999, p. xix.

64. U.S. troop strength from "Key Facts and Figures," available from *www.nato.int/kfor/*.

65. *America's Role in Nation Building, From Germany to Iraq*, Santa Monica, CA: Rand Corporation, 2003, p. 126.

66. Clinton, *My Life*, p. 859.

67. Daalder and Michael O'Hanlon, *Winning Ugly*, p. 1.

68. Quoted in "Crisis in the Balkans; Statements of United States Policy on Kosovo," *New York Times*, April 19, 1999, available from *www.nytimes.com/1999/04/18/world/crisis-in-the-balkans-statements-of-united-states-policy-on-kosovo.html*.

69. *Ibid.*

70. David P. Auerswald, "Explaining Wars of Choice: An Integrated Decision Model of NATO Policy in Kosovo," *International Studies Quarterly*, Vol. 48, No. 3, September 2004, p. 648.

71. President William J. Clinton, "Address to the Nation," March 24, 1999, available from *www.pbs.org/newshour/bb/europe/jan-june99/address_3-24.html*.

72. *Ibid.*

73. Carole Rogel, " Kosovo: Where It All Began," *International Journal of Politics, Culture, and Society*, Vol. 17, No. 1, Fall, 2003, p. 178.

74. "Explaining Wars of Choice," p. 646.

75. Daalder and O'Hanlon, *Winning Ugly*, p. 5.

76. *Ibid.*, pp. 2-3.

77. UN Security Resolution 1244, S/RES/1244, 1999, June 10, 1999.

78. "NATO's Role in Kosovo," KFOR Homepage, available from *www.nato.int/cps/en/natolive/topics_48818.htm*.

79. Troops strength, *Kosovo/Kosova: As Seen, as Told,* Vol. II, Vienna, Austria: Office of Security and Cooperation in Europe, December 1999, p. xix.

80. U.S. troops strength from "Key Facts and Figures," available from *www.nato.int/kfor/*.

81. UN Security Council Resolution, S/RES/1970, 2011, February 26, 2011.

82. UN Security Council Resolution, S/RES/1973, 2011, March 17, 2011.

83. "UN Res 1973 [does] not Sanction Interference in Civil War in Libya," *Tass/Itar*, March 28, 2011.

84. "NATO Operations in Libya: data journalism breaks down which country does what," *Guardian*, (UK) data blog, available from *www.guardian.co.uk/news/datablog/2011/may/22/nato-libya-data-journalism-operations-country*.

85. Gent, "Going in When it Counts," pp. 713-735.

86. Robert Gates, quoted in "No-Fly Zone for Libya would Require Attack," *Reuters* online, *www.reuters.com/article/2011/03/02/us-libya-usa-pentagon-idUSTRE7214EX20110302*.

87. Matt Gurney, "Why America won't bomb Libya; Eliminating Gaddafi's air force would involve the U.S. in a potential civil war and commit it to further action," *National Post*, Canada, February 24, 2011, p. A18.

88. President Barack Obama, "Remarks by the President in Address to the Nation on Libya," March 28, 2011, available from *www.whitehouse.gov/the-press-office/2011/03/28/remarks-president-address-nation-libya*.

89. Fareed Zakaria, "Why are we in Libya? *Time*, Vol. 177, Issue 13, April 4, 2011, pp. 32-35.

90. Nicolas Sarkozy quoted in Stephen Erlanger, "French Aid Bolsters Libyan Revolt," *New York Times* on the web, February 28, 2011, available from *www.nytimes.com/2011/03/01/world/europe/01france.html?_r=1*.

91. Kim Wilsher, "As France Takes the Reigns on Libya, Sarkozy Triumphs," *Los Angeles Times* online, March 20, 2011, available from *articles.latimes.com/2011/mar/20/world/la-fg-libya-sarkozy-20110320*.

92. Michael Elliot, "How Libya became a French and British War," *Time* online, March 19, 2011, available from *www.time.com/time/world/article/0,8599,2060412,00.html.*

93. *Leave None to Tell the Story: Genocide in Rwanda,* Human Rights Watch Report, March 1999, available from *www.hrw.org/legacy/reports/1999/rwanda/Geno1-3-04.htm#P95_39230.*

94. Romeo Dallaire Interview, "Ghosts of Rwanda," April 1, 2004, available from *www.pbs.org/wgbh/pages/frontline/shows/ghosts/interviews/dallaire.html.*

95. George Moose, "Crisis in Rwanda," U.S. Department of State Dispatch, Vol. 5, Issue 21, May 23, 1994, p. 342.

96. See Alan J. Kuperman, "Rwanda in Retrospect," *Foreign Affairs,* Vol. 79, Issue 1, January/February 2000, pp. 94-118.

97. *Ibid.,* p. 101.

98. *Special Report of the Secretary-General on the United Nations Assistance Mission for Rwanda,* UN Document, S/1994/470, April 20, 1994.

99. *Report of the Secretary General on the Situation in Rwanda,* UN Document, S/1994/565, May 13, 1994.

100. Joshua Hamer and Theodore Stranger, "Deeper into the Abyss," *Newsweek,* Vol. 123, Issue 17, April 25, 1994, pp. 32-33.

101. *Ibid.,* p. 33; Kuperman says that the quote comes from a letter written by Dallaire on April 15, "Rwanda in Retrospect," p. 102.

102. *Ibid.,* pp. 105-110.

103. *Ibid.,* p. 108.

104. Stephen Wertheim, "A Solution from Hell: The United States and the Rise of Humanitarian Interventionism, 1991–2003," *Journal of Genocide Research,* Vol. 12, Nos. 3-4, September-December 2010, pp. 149-172.

105. For a detailed discussion of these groups, see Joseph Holliday, *Middle East Security Report Number 3: Syria's Armed Opposition*, Washington, DC: Institute for the Study of War, 2012.

106. "Guide: Syria Crisis," *BBC World News* Online, available from *www.bbc.co.uk/news/world-middle-east-15936813*.

107. "Syrian Death Toll Tops 19,000, Say Activists," *The Guardian* UK) Online, July 22, 2012, available from *www.guardian.co.uk/world/2012/jul/22/syria-death-toll-tops-19000*.

108. "Syria Regional Refugee Response," UNHCR Website, updated August 15, 2012, available from *data.unhcr.org/syrianrefugees/regional.php*.

109. Adel Darwish, "Scan Prospects of International Intervention," *The Middle East*, May 2012, p. 21.

110. Sara A. Carter, "U.S.: Al Qaeda, other extremists aiding Syrian rebels," *The Washington Examiner* Online, August 9, 2012, available from *washingtonexaminer.com/u.s.-al-qaeda-other-extremists-aiding-syrian-rebels/article/2504501*.

111. BBC News Interview with Secretary of State Hillary Clinton, available from *www.bbc.co.uk/news/world-middle-east-17170775*.

112. "The Syrian Dilemma," *The Nation*, Vol. 294, Nos. 10, 11, March 5/12, 2012, p. 3.

113. Fred Anderson and Andrew Cayton, *The Dominion of War: Empire and Liberty in North America, 1500-2000*, New York: Penguin, 2005, p. xviii.

114. See Kreps, "The 1994 Haiti Intervention: A Unilateral Operation in Multilateral Clothes."

115. *Joint Publication 3-57: Civil-Military Operations*, Washington, DC: 2008, p. I-8.

116. "Public Wary of Military Intervention in Libya," Pew Research Center Publications, March 14, 2011, available from *pewresearch.org/pubs/1927/strong-opposition-us-involvement-libya-military-overcommitted.*

117. *Ibid.*

118. *Ibid.*

119. Carolyn J. Logan, "Public Support and the Intervention in Somalia: Lessons for the Future of Military-Humanitarian Interventions," *The Fletcher Forum of World Affairs,* Vol. 2012, Summer/Fall 1996, p. 160.

120. *Ibid.,* p. 156.

121. Matthew A. Baum, "How Public Opinion Constrains the Use of Force: The Case of Operation Restore Hope," *Presidential Studies Quarterly,* Vol. 34, No. 2, June 2004, pp. 1887-2226.

122. See Frank G. Hoffman, *Conflict in the 21st Century: the Rise of Hybrid Wars,* Arlington, VA: Potomac Institute, 2007.

123. *Quadrennial Defense Review Report,* Washington, DC: Department of Defense, 2010, p. x.

124. Nathan Freier, *The New Balance: Limited Armed Stabilization and the Future of U.S. Landpower,* Carlisle, PA: Strategic Studies Institute, U.S. Army War College, 2009, p. vii.

125. *Quadrennial Defense Review Report,* p. 20.

126. *Ibid.,* p. 24.

127. *The New Balance,* p. 10.

128. Antulio Echeveria, *Preparing for One War and Getting Another?* Carlisle, PA: Strategic Studies Institute, U.S. Army War College, 2010.